CAMBRIDGE LIBRARY COLLECTION

Books of enduring scholarly value

History

The books reissued in this series include accounts of historical events and movements by eye-witnesses and contemporaries, as well as landmark studies that assembled significant source materials or developed new historiographical methods. The series includes work in social, political and military history on a wide range of periods and regions, giving modern scholars ready access to influential publications of the past.

Travels in Spain and the East, 1808–1810

The son of Erasmus Darwin and uncle of Charles Darwin, Francis Darwin lived a mostly quiet life as a doctor in Lichfield, taking early retirement to a remote part of Derbyshire. As a young man, however, he took an intrepid and eventful Grand Tour of the Mediterranean and kept a detailed journal. The quick succession of places and events and the constant danger due to war, piracy and plague make this a thrilling read, with murder and adventure on every page. Highlights of the journey include a mountain climb with a bottle of laudanum as the only provision, a daring escape over the rooftops of a Greek village from a group of enraged natives, and dinner with Lord Byron, though Darwin frustratingly reveals little about the poet. The journal was edited for publication by his grandson in 1927, in 'tribute to the remarkable pluck and indomitable energy of the author'.

Travels in Spain and the East, 1808–1810

Francis Sacheverell Darwin
Edited by Francis Swift Darwin

CAMBRIDGE UNIVERSITY PRESS

Cambridge New York Melbourne Madrid Cape Town Singapore São Paolo Delhi

Published in the United States of America by Cambridge University Press, New York

www.cambridge.org
Information on this title: www.cambridge.org/9781108004312

This edition first published 1927
This digitally printed version 2009

ISBN 978-1-108-00431-2

TRAVELS
IN
SPAIN AND THE EAST

CAMBRIDGE
UNIVERSITY PRESS
LONDON: Fetter Lane

NEW YORK
The Macmillan Co.
BOMBAY, CALCUTTA and MADRAS
Macmillan and Co., Ltd.
TORONTO
The Macmillan Co. of Canada, Ltd.
TOKYO
Maruzen-Kabushiki-Kaisha

SIR FRANCIS SACHEVERELL DARWIN
(1786–1859)

TRAVELS IN SPAIN AND THE EAST

1808–1810

by

Sir Francis Sacheverell Darwin

Cambridge
AT THE UNIVERSITY PRESS
1927

PRINTED IN GREAT BRITAIN

IN PIAM MEMORIAM

GEORGIANAE E. DARWIN

Filiae Dilectae, Matris Amantissimae

MEMOIR

THE AUTHOR of this diary, Francis Sacheverell Darwin, was born on 17 June 1786—being the sixth son of the scientist and poet, Erasmus Darwin of Lichfield. He was educated at Repton School and Emmanuel College, Cambridge, and took the degree of M.D. at Edinburgh. From 1808 to 1810 he saw something of the world in the tour described in these pages—in the company of Theodore Galton, uncle of the well-known biologist Sir Francis Galton. After his return Dr Darwin practised as a physician at Lichfield; and in 1815 he married Jane Harriett Ryle, daughter of John Ryle of Macclesfield. He was knighted on 10 May 1820 at Carlton House, by George IV—on his presenting to the new sovereign an address from the City of Lichfield. Sir Francis is said to have had the best practice in the neighbourhood of Lichfield; but he gave it up from his intense love of country life, and went in 1822 or 1823 to reside at Sydnope Hall, near Darley Dale, Derbyshire; and in 1847 he removed to Breadsall Priory, near Derby, where he died on 6 November 1859—deeply lamented by his family, and by friends both rich and poor.

He left ten children, one of whom writes: "In personal appearance, as well as in mind, my father had few equals. He was 6 feet 3 inches in height, with a fine figure and a remarkably handsome and intellectual face. He was deeply endowed with classical and varied knowledge of all kinds"—to which the obituary notice in the *Annual Register* of 1859 (p. 419) adds that he "ranked high in scientific attainments, inheriting his father's literary tastes and distinguished abilities."

The following pages have been reproduced from Lady Darwin's copy of her husband's diary—or, rather, from a transcript of that copy made at considerable trouble and expense by Mr B. Ryle Swift, one of her grandsons. Another—the undersigned—has done the editing, *i.e.* reduced but not altered the text, left untouched certain irregularities of spelling, modernised the punctuation, and added one or two footnotes and a pedigree. While we may regret that Sir Francis did not always utilise his opportunities (why, for instance, did he not put on record his impressions of Lord Byron?), still the journal gives a vivid illustration of the dangers of travel in the days of the Peninsular War, and is in itself a tribute to the remarkable pluck and indomitable energy of the author.

F. D. S. DARWIN

January 1927

CONTENTS

CHAPTER I

CORUNNA, ST JAGO, VIGO, OPORTO

November and December, 1808

I LEFT Breadsall Priory in Derbyshire on Sunday morning November 20th 1808, and slept that night and the following at Birmingham. On Tuesday the 22nd, with my friend Mr Theo. Galton, I proceeded to Falmouth, where on Saturday the 26th we found the packet for Corunna was about to sail in two hours. Being provided with passports from the Secretary of State's Office, and having paid 20 guineas each for our passage to Corunna, we embarked in the Express Packet, Capt. Sampson, and weighed anchor at 10 o'clock the same morning.

Our society on this voyage consisted of a well-informed man, a Mr Arbuthnot, who had formerly held some civil appointment at Ceylon; Mr Clarke, who had belonged to the Army, and now went as a Volunteer into the Spanish Service; and Mr Adey, a young gentleman on his way to join Sir J. Moore's regiment, the 52nd. T. G. and myself now became more acquainted every hour; and on this voyage we formed a most sincere friendship, which increased and strengthened as our dispositions were better known to each other.

The wind was favourable; and in the space of a day and night we were in the midst of the Bay of Biscay. Here it was we first experienced a heavy sea; and the waves running mountains high now raised us above, and now appeared to engulf our ship in the bosom of the deep.

During the obscure light of parting day we reflected on the uncertainty of human events, and occasionally conversed upon the change we had chosen—from the quiet comforts of an English home, to a country involved in all the miseries of War.

The gale increased towards midnight; and all hands on board were actively employed until morning in making everything secure and keeping the pumps at work. As the morning dawned we found ourselves very near to a large ship, which proved to be a Spanish merchantman—greatly to our satisfaction, for the Captain suspected her intentions were not very friendly, and we had in a great hurry made the vessel ready for action: the appearance of our brig had also inspired the Spaniards with a corresponding terror, and we spoke each other with all our guns ready to fire at the word of command.

We continued to toss about this vast bay for two or three days, during one of which the wind entirely died away and our ship rolled amongst the heavy swell. Towards mid-day a fine turtle asleep on the waves attracted our attention, and the Captain expected to catch him—but we had no such treat as Turtle soup on this voyage.

At 5 o'clock p.m. on Wednesday the 30th we had

the happiness of once more setting our feet on terra firma at Corunna. Here we found everything in confusion from its vicinity to the Army, which was at this time about 30 miles from the City; and it was with difficulty we obtained even chairs to sleep upon at the Leo d'Oro. It was impossible to return to our vessel, or to get on board any other, in consequence of the embarkation and disembarkation of soldiers and stores. The "Tonnant," 84 guns, is the Flag-ship at present in this place; she was taken at the Battle of the Nile, and was the last in the French Service which struck to Lord Nelson.

Mr Clarke went on in the evening to St Jago de Compostella—having understood that some Spaniards were in arms at that place, and wishing to join their detachment against the enemy. We took leave of Messrs Arbuthnot and Adey; and on the 4th December—each mounted on a stubborn mule, for which we paid ten dollars—we proceeded on the road to St Jago early in the morning, over a dreary tract of country of 40 miles, and a great part of the journey only distant a few miles from the French outposts. We became more reconciled to the cold and wildness of the scenery as the evening closed in; and it was dark when we arrived at a Posada in the City.

On the following morning we delivered a letter of introduction, given to us by our bankers in Corunna—MM. Riberas—to Mr Saldarini, an Italian gentleman, whose civilities during our stay were unbounded. Mr Saldarini informed us of the melancholy fate of poor Mr Clarke, who had been robbed and murdered the night before: we could not gain any local information about the remains of our unhappy friend, and never afterwards heard more of him.

Our Italian friend informed us that a beautiful young English girl was in a convent in the next street, and that the laws of this nunnery would permit us to speak with her if we would aver that we were related to the poor girl—which we did not hesitate to assert, and thus arrived within the precincts of this solitary abode. Charlotte Glasgow appeared in the melancholy costume of a Spanish nun, and in company with an old abbess: she informed us that five years had elapsed since the time in which she left her mother's care and eloped with a Spanish captain, who brought her to St Jago, and himself died four days afterwards of a dreadful fever, leaving her destitute of food and friends. We spent above an hour in conversation with this poor girl, and every moment made us more interested in her cause: we gave her all the tea out of our canteen, and left money for the convent.

Lord Holland, whom we found with his lady at Corunna on our arrival there, followed us to this City—where we offered him the use of our rooms at the Inn; and in return he presented us with a bottle of excellent Claret.

On the 6th December we left St Jago, and after

a tedious journey of 40 miles reached Pontevedra at about 6 o'clock in the evening. Here the accommodations were bad, as at the preceding Posada (or inn)—where we had been much annoyed with mosquitos. This day we hired only two mules—one for our baggage, and the other carried us alternately; and thus we diminished our expenses, and had besides a variety of exercise. The town of Pontevedra is small, poor, ill-built, and uninteresting.

7th December—Our journey was short; and with much pleasure we entered the town of Vigo, where most of the Transports rendezvous to receive the Army in case of retreat. After dinner we walked to a monastery with Signor Francisco, a Portuguese gentleman, who was very polite at the table d'hote. He introduced us to the Abbot, who had little to exhibit except a fine prospect of mountains and the Harbour. On returning from our walk we found the town in the greatest alarm in consequence of an appearance on the road from Pontevedra which the inhabitants had magnified into the bright helmets of retreating soldiers—until with the aid of our telescopes we discovered it to be the reflection of the sun upon the windows of Lord Holland's carriage!

At Vigo we again procured two mules; and in company with Signor Francisco, who conversed with us in French, we proceeded to Iny—a town situated near the river Minho, which divides Spain from Portugal in this part. The distance was about

16 miles, and here the passports were obtained to cross the river; but no sooner had we reached the other side, than a guard of soldiers marched us as prisoners to a small fort on the summit of a hill commanding the passage of the Minho. Signor Francisco had accidentally spoken a few words of French in the boat—which was the cause of our being arrested; and the Governor told us it was well we were not killed—so great is the hatred of the Spaniards to the French. Our passports explained everything satisfactorily; but, as we had been so long detained and the day was far advanced, we slept that night in the garrison.

At 5 o'clock in the morning—having as usual been almost devoured during the night, and the draw-bridges, gates, etc. of this little fortress being opened—we sallied forth for the town of Viana, and reached it at 7 in the evening. Viana is a pleasant little town full of convents, some of them fine buildings: for want of a better lodging we were obliged to sleep in a dirty kitchen with 12 or 14 other people on a stone floor. The next morning leaving the town at 6 o'clock, and despairing of any comfort, we descried a nice clean coffee-house already open; and in the enjoyment of an excellent breakfast on coffee we forgot the miseries of the preceding night. On resuming our march we passed through Barcellos to an inn on the road about 16 miles from Oporto, and here for the first time made use of our bags to sleep in. These tied round the neck, and thus entirely enclosing the body, kept it from the mosquitos, etc.

11th December—The roads on this day's journey we found very heavy and sandy, the country mountainous and covered with thick forests of pine. Upon some of the trees we were surprised to see little girls of about 10 years old cutting wood at the height of 60 to 80 feet from the ground. At a house where we stopped on the road we observed a Spanish doctor bleeding a Portuguese officer, who had fallen from his horse; and, having lacerated his patient's arm and succeeded in drawing blood, to our great surprise he tasted it, with a most mysterious countenance—in order, as he informed us, to ascertain the extent of the injury received by the fall!

As we approached Oporto the country assumed a more cultivated appearance; but torrents of rain rendered the latter part of our journey very uncomfortable. Oporto is a fine town containing a population of about 60,000 inhabitants. It is situated on a hill upon one side of which the houses descend to the river, and extend along its banks to a great distance: over the Douro is a bridge of boats, well constructed, which rise and fall according to the tide. This communicates with the small town on the opposite side of the river—the entrance to which is very bad owing to a dangerous Bar or sand-bank, which at low water is nearly exposed; and very few ships of any description now harbour here. The wine of Oporto is expressed from the grape about

16 leagues up the river, where are hills entirely covered with vineyards: it is brought down to market, and sold in one day to the numerous merchants of Oporto. About 30,000 pipes are sent annually to England.

Our lodgings were at a comfortable house in the Rue des Angleses; and we dined every day in company with a Captain Daubrava and a Mr Gooden, a very polite merchant.

At Oporto there is a good Opera house, but not so large as Covent Garden Theatre. The performance is comparatively very poor, especially in the ballets: one female only, Mme Angelina, in dancing, afforded any amusement. The inhabitants, in going to the Theatre, are always accompanied by a man with a flambeau to prevent murder, which is so constantly perpetrated in the streets. I saw one poor fellow whose side was actually laid open by a stiletto. Yesterday above 40 men were taken up, and executed on suspicion of treason: many of them died with great bravery. In walking with Captain Daubrava to-day we saved a Frenchman from an infuriated mob, who were pursuing the poor fellow to death. His gratitude to us in consequence was so great, that even the weather-beaten countenance of our brave German friend[1] could not refrain from tears.

Since leaving Corunna there has not been a drop of rain excepting on our arrival at Oporto. Fahren-

[[1] Presumably Captain Daubrava. F. D. S. D.]

heit's thermometer stood yesterday at 2 o'clock at 58° in the shade. There are at present several hundred wounded English soldiers, who are daily sent to Oporto from the Army to embark for England.

CHAPTER II

LISBON AND CINTRA

December 1808—January 1809

DECEMBER 19TH: We left Oporto; and on this day's journey of four leagues we overtook a Spanish sailor—a man of colour, his name Raphael. He had been in the English Service, and was useful to us as an interpreter. We slept at a dirty posada —where we should have been murdered, if our friend the black had not awakened us and pressed our immediate departure, in consequence of our interfering with the landlord who had been beating his wife.

We proceeded 7 leagues over a barren country. The muleteer and his son, who accompanied us, smoked their pipes, sung 'Viva Rey Fernando,' and crossed themselves before several monuments of travellers who had died or been killed in these deserts. About half way to Coimbra we met about 40 carts, drawn by oxen, and escorted by part of the 38th Regiment, with provisions for Salamanca.

We arrived at Coimbra about 2 o'clock on the 21st December. The afternoon we spent in resting at the posada, being a good deal fatigued after the day's journey, and but little inclined to explore the town: however, on the following day the highest point above the City was our object, to obtain a prospect of the whole. Coimbra stands on very uneven ground, and nearly surrounded by the river Mondego; it looks better at a distance than when you are in its streets. The museum of the College, and the Convent of Santa Cruz, are well worth visiting. The monks, some of whom speak French, are extremely civil: they have a magnificent chapel nearly equal to the Cathedral of St Jago.

Leaving our friend Francisco at Coimbra, we proceeded on the road to Lisbon in a kind of curricle, the rainy season having set in—our black friend attending us on foot. Seven leagues brought us to Pombal, passing through a second detachment of the Army. Pombal is a village of good size; and on a neighbouring hill stands a fine ruin of an ancient fortress that has seen better times. In the Hall of this castle now lies the coffin of its late occupier, which has lain there a number of years, without the proper respect of a son being paid to his father's remains: years roll on, and this wretch has never forgiven the former persecutions of his parent[1].

From hence on the following morning we went on four leagues to the beautiful little University of Leiria. It was a most delightful day; and the bells of

[[1] This statement can hardly refer to the body of the well-known Portuguese statesman, the Marquis of Pombal (1699–1782) who seems to have lived and died on perfectly good terms with his two sons—though it is possible that his interment may have been prevented by the Portuguese government, which imprisoned the priest who pronounced his funeral oration, and ordered the distinctly provocative epitaph to be erased from his monument. Cf. J. Smith, *Memoirs of the Marquis of Pombal*, vol. II. pp. 366–8 (London, 1843). F. D. S. D.]

the different colleges were ringing as we entered the town. This University, in consequence of the sad pressure of war, is now almost entirely deserted—a few students only refusing to join the general cause against the tyrannical invaders. This town has since been entirely consumed by fire by the French, who, retreating through the valley, thus thought to stay the pursuing forces.

After resting at this charming spot, we passed on three leagues farther to Carvallos for the night, and found miserable accommodations in a large, lonely, wretched posada, full of nocturnal vermin.

The Elements next morning seemed to threaten destruction to our vehicle: one of our mules fell in going down a steep hill, and we were thrown to the ground with great violence, but fortunately escaped without much injury—not, however, without being completely soaked by the rain. Five leagues this stormy day brought us to Rio Major, where our lodgings for the night were better than usual.

The next morning, intending to sleep at Villa Franca, we passed on; but, coming to a house two miles short of it, the inhabitants told us that a powerful banditti of deserters from the Army haunted the road that very afternoon, and had shot and robbed some Spaniards passing that way. Thinking it therefore more prudent to halt, we secured the house as well as we could, and kept watch alternately two hours each during the night. Next morning the black, with a blunderbuss which we had told him to fire as a signal of the enemy's being in sight, preceded us through the wood to Villa Franca, where we breakfasted on fish and olives; then travelling on six leagues we at length arrived at Lisbon on the 27th December, a good deal worn with the fatigues of our journey by land all the way from Corunna.

Many congratulations mutually took place on meeting with Mr Arbuthnot, who had come by water from that place: here we also found Mr Gooden, who had sailed round from Oporto. Comfortable lodgings were to be had at Mrs Callaman's, No. 30, opposite to the Convent of St Francisco. Mr Setaro, to whom we had a letter of introduction from Lord Robert Fitzgerald, rendered our stay in Lisbon very agreeable.

This large City abounds with a species of Dog without tails and without owners: they are very savage, and always defend each other if insulted. It is said that the French destroyed upward of 5,000 of these animals, which from their numbers were considered a great nuisance. The beggars in this grand city are almost as numerous as the dogs: what is so disagreeable, they are allowed to infest the best coffee-houses and even to beg at the table, and it is no uncommon thing for them to sit down with you at meals and afterwards to beg.

Sunday, 1st January 1809, we visited Cintra, distant 20 miles, in a curricle: although it rained all day, we hoped for the following one being fine

—and so it was. Signor Cavigioli was our host at this place: he had married an Irishwoman, and we were as comfortable as at an English inn.

Cintra contains about 200 houses and 1,500 inhabitants. It is situated chiefly on a small hill in the side of a range or chain of mountains: the beauty of the place consists in its position in those hills, which extend about 10 miles towards the sea, where they are known by sailors under the name of The Rocks of Lisbon. They are covered with woods of Cork, Pine, and Oranges, amongst which are situated the numerous Kintras or country houses. Opposite to this range of rocks are extensive and dreary wastes: these, perhaps by their contrasts, tend to heighten the beauty of the scenery about Cintra.

The palace here is a very large building: it may indeed rather be said to consist of a number of small houses joined together. In a small room they exhibit the throne of Don Sebastian, king of Portugal: it is constructed of small blue tiles, the back being formed by the wall. The dungeon also is to be seen where Don Alfonso[1] was confined for 9 years, and in which he died: the tiles in one part of the cell are much worn by his frequent walking to and fro on that spot. There is a curious bath also, or room where the water plays upon those within from every part of the chamber, resembling the Temple of Water at Chatsworth.

Another palace, belonging to the Marquis de

[[1] Alfonso VI, deposed in 1667, died in 1675. F. D. S. D.]

Romellio, is situated on a height nearly corresponding to that on which Cintra stands, and about a mile from it. Here the unfortunate convention after the Battle of Vimeira was signed; and it is about 14 miles from that field of blood. There are on the rock above the Town some extensive remains of an ancient Moorish castle: a curious bath is found here —so clear that one of the party actually stepped into the water without supposing it to be full at the time. On the same height is a Convent inhabited by five poor old monks: the building is large, and once contained above thirty of them.

Mounted on donkeys we visited Mafra, distant 14 miles: it is a large Convent, formerly containing some hundred of monks, but their number is now reduced to 40. 6,000 French soldiers slept in it the night before the Battle of Vimeira, and nearly destroyed a valuable library. From hence we walked to the field of blood, where we observed many unburied bones. The guide desired us to remark eight human skeletons lying in a vineyard—half of them were said to be English, the others Frenchmen: owing to the foliage at the time, these bodies had escaped being buried.

Having enjoyed the neighbourhood of Cintra, we returned to Lisbon on the 4th January—resolved to take the first opportunity that might offer of a vessel to Cadiz, being tired of travelling by land.

The next day we resorted to the British Factory burying ground. This is a most interesting spot: it contains 218 monuments—many of them sacred to the memory of those unfortunate young persons who, as having been consumptive, were sent here for change of climate. Three English officers' wives have died here lately; and many soldiers who fought on the 21st August, and afterwards died of their wounds, are also buried here. The place is full of Cypress trees, which cast a melancholy shade over it; and under them are found many elegant tombstones. Fielding, the author, is, I believe, buried here[1].

At dinner we became acquainted with a medical man, who assured me that he had seen the eight soldiers above mentioned at Vimeira about a week after the battle, and that two of the English and one of the Frenchmen had not been mortally wounded, but had bled to death.

A return of the officers, who have perished on the retreat towards Corunna from Salamanca, has just been received: amongst the unfortunate men we are truly grieved to see poor Mr Adey's name. It appears he expired from fatigue: thus another of our original party has perished.

At the foot of the Eastern hill of Lisbon we still find many houses in the same dilapidated state in which they were left after the great earthquake[2]. Part of the town, which was thus destroyed, con-

[[1] The novelist (1707–54)—to whom a monument was erected in this cemetery in 1830. F. D. S. D.]

[[2] Of 1 November 1755. F. D. S. D.]

sisted of very large houses in poor, narrow, and dirty streets—which have since been restored on a very different and more commodious scale, with many fine and handsome buildings.

The Plazza di Commercio is a large and elegant square, 600 feet × 550 feet, with an equestrian statue of Don Josef in bronze on a pedestal of stone in the centre. Three very extensive and well-built streets lead from the square. At the further end of the centre of these streets is situated the Palace of the Inquisition, which is supposed at this moment to contain some few unhappy persons lingering in chains and torture.

Great activity is used in training young recruits for the Army; and we observe in most of the streets large companies of soldiers who appear to be the whole day drilling, except when the bells call them to Mass—and this happens very frequently in the day. Some English officers superintend different regiments, which are daily marched off to the Armies and replaced by young recruits.

Accounts of frequent murders arrive daily from the road towards Oporto, and it is thought wonderful how we have escaped.

CHAPTER III

CADIZ, XERES, SEVILLE

January and February 1809

16TH JANUARY.—The wind being fair we sailed for Cadiz in the "General Wolfe" Merchant ship, Captain Bound, having as companions Messrs Arbuthnot, Gooden, Bailey, Knutzen, and a Mr Poppe. Here, in a noisome ship of fish from Newfoundland, did we toss about the Atlantic until Sunday the 22nd. Having doubled Cape St Vincent, the first thing to attract our notice was a fine turtle asleep on the waves; but he escaped being taken. The next day a large whale entertained us by his mode of throwing up the water, at no great distance from the ship. It was midnight when, in the direction that our captain expected to make Cadiz, a light appeared which he mistook for the lighthouse near the town. The ship was then going eight knots an hour and we did not seem to gain upon the light, which shortly afterwards disappeared—and we heard the breakers upon the shore, which greatly alarmed the crew. Captain Bound now put the vessel about, with her head towards the stream; for we found ourselves drawing fast with the current into the straits of Gibraltar. When daylight appeared, the Captain was convinced that—had not this been done at the moment—we must inevitably have been wrecked. The wind, changing a point, brought us safely to anchor in the Bay of Cadiz.

Admiral Purvis's boat immediately came to enquire what news we brought; but of this we gave and received but little. Presently afterwards a Don arrived from the town in a sixteen-oared barge, desiring us to perform quarantine. However, at 6 o'clock the following day a happy release arrived; and 23rd January we found ourselves safe within the walls of Wood's American Hotel. Mr Duff, the English Consul, has resided about 50 years at Cadiz. He obligingly invited us to dinner; and our party consisted of Sir G. Smith, who was then in a consumptive state, Mr Slade, also in the same unhappy situation and travelling for his health, Sir William Ingilby, Mr Mackinnon, Captain Pickering from Gibraltar, Mr Arbuthnot, Major Browne, and ourselves. No sooner was dinner over than a Spanish marquis and his daughter were announced; and the young lady took her glass as freely as any of us, although she had no female companion. Having sat about half-an-hour discussing politics, we retired into another apartment for coffee; and, directly after this, each took a glass of Noyeau or Cherry Brandy, and then took leave of our kind host.

January 26th.—We walked about the town, and visited the Cathedral. The Bull Amphitheatre next demanded our attention; but the sport is seldom now continued. The fortifications of the City are very extensive, and the situation of Cadiz is naturally strong: new batteries are nevertheless forming along the Isthmus.

On walking about a mile out of the town, our attention was directed to the sight of four dead Frenchmen, who were about to be buried by as many live ones in chains, guarded by some Spanish soldiers. The unfortunate prisoners died in the Hospital; and, as the Spaniards will not touch or bury them when dead, the living French invalids are obliged to perform this last office for their departed comrades. On conversing with one of the grave diggers, he informed us that one of the bodies—at the same time striking it with his spade—was his brother, and spoke of it in the most hardened and unfeeling manner. There are at this time about 9,000 prisoners of war[1] in the ships at Cadiz—exclusive of those who die in the hospital on land: all the bodies are thrown overboard without even a weight attached to sink them, shot being considered too expensive for the purpose. Hence it is dreadful to see numbers of dead bodies floating about the harbour, and washed on shore—there to infest the air; for they are neither interred, nor again given to the deep. We saw 13 bodies washed up together in one creek of the Bay. From five to fifteen daily expire on board the ships from disease and famine; and about five die each day in the hospital, chiefly young men.

[[1] These were the prisoners taken at Baylen on 22 July 1808—when the French general Dupont capitulated with his army to the Spaniards under Castaños. F. D. S. D.]

On Monday 30th January, having procured the necessary passports, we left Cadiz in a small boat to overtake a larger that was crossing the Bay to Port St Mary's, and after a short row accomplished this; but, on coming alongside of her, we had great difficulty in persuading the boatman who had command of the vessel to take us in, and at the same time there was very apparent confusion in all their countenances. The party consisted of five sailors, a poor woman, and a Spanish ship's Captain, with ourselves. The sea ran very high, and the nearer we approached the Bar (a rock which stretches across the Bay on going to Port St Mary's, and is at low water seen in part) we observed a tremendous surge, caused by the very extensive sweep of the Atlantic in this situation; and the increasing alarm of our crew was too evident not to convince us of our immediate peril. It was too late to return: we approached the spot, to be carried over on an enormous wave—which, swelling as it rolled, lifted our little bark on high, and in one instant burst upon the rock; each succeeding breaker filled our boat, now sinking fast, and we clinging to it. Then indeed did we give ourselves up as lost; but it was decreed otherwise. A sudden squall upon the sails righted the boat again—and we had crossed the Bar, and each baled out the water with his hat. We at length reached the shore, and thanked God for our miraculous preservation. Upon arriving at Port St Mary's we received much kindness and attention from Mr Ryan, who provided us with dry clothing, etc.

Our course at night was directed, in a Phaeton and four, to Xeres—only eleven miles distant, and on the way to Seville: here by calling upon a Mr Gordon, the great Sherry wine merchant, we met with great civility. His house was in some confusion, from having lost two servants by the effect of confined charcoal fire in their sleeping room the preceding night. I had the curiosity to examine the bodies, which were nearly black—as though they had been strangled. This place and neighbourhood produces the best Sherry wine, called Pagaretti or Paciaretti, from the Spanish word "Pago" a district. About 1,800 vines are planted on an acre, and a good year produces about 3 butts per acre. Most of the wine vaults were bricked up in the expectation of their being plundered by the French; and I have since understood that many of them were discovered by the enemy bribing some of the worst people of Xeres to direct their search.

It was now 12 o'clock at night, and a beautiful full moon invited us to advance. It is usual for foreigners to hire some dragoons to protect them; but, having left our baggage at Cadiz, we had little to fear and nothing to lose. Having slept part of the night, and the other part watched for robbers, our sight was gratified with a pleasing view of Seville; and at 3 o'clock p.m. we found accommodations, poor as they were, at the Posada del Sol.

Seville is a large town, containing about 60,000 inhabitants; and about 15,000 have been added since the French took Madrid. Here the Grand Junta sit; and here our ambassador, Mr Frere, resides.

The next morning, February 1st, we visited the Convent of St Jerome—a league from Seville—in company with Sir William Ingilby and Mr Mackinnon, who had arrived the day before. Here to our great satisfaction we saw the famous General Castanos[1], who is confined under suspicions of treason. He is very polite, speaks French fluently, and pressed us much to dine with him.

The Cathedral is a fine building, 420 feet by 263 and 126 in height: it was built in 1401 and contains 80 painted glass windows. In the centre of the Church is a monument to Christopher Columbus, on which are represented two galleys steering to the coast of the New World. The body of Florida Blanca[2] now lies in great state in the Church: he was the late President of the Supreme Junta—an old man, and much beloved.

[[1] Born on 22 April 1756—four days after the French landing in Minorca began the Seven Years' War—and died on 24 September 1852—ten days after the death of Wellington, who himself was born in 1769. It was to Castaños that the French general Dupont capitulated on 22 July 1808 at Baylen —after the first battle of the Peninsular War. F. D. S. D.]

[[2] The Spanish statesman, who died on 20 November 1808. F. D. S. D.]

The Tobacco Manufactory is a large building, which employs 500 men; and 12,000 weight of the Rappe Snuff is said to be prepared monthly. The Cannon Foundry is the largest in Spain, and they finish 24 pieces every month: 100 men are employed, and we were so fortunate as to see them cast nine 32-pounders of brass.

Having delivered our letter of introduction from Lord Robert Fitzgerald, we had the honour of dining with Mr Frere—whom we found extremely reserved on the subject of the movements of the Armies, now in the most interesting stage of the campaign.

We left Seville on the 4th; and, sleeping at Xeres, the next day we arrived at Port St Mary's. On the way we saw upon the plains some bustards nearly 7 feet high, but could not get near enough to shoot one of them. It was low tide and impossible to cross the Bar again—on which account we proceeded round the Bay and through Isola by land to Cadiz, when we arrived at its gates at 2 o'clock. The City of Cadiz is under Military law; and, if half-a-dozen of the inhabitants are collected together in the streets, they are immediately dispersed. The fortifications are repairing and new ones making, to resist the enemy—about whose movements there appears the greatest ignorance, as no one dares communicate any information at the Coffee-houses.

The house of the Marquis de Solano, which stands fronting the Sea, is an object of interest to the fresh arriver. The mob had turned two of the heavy guns of the Battery upon this house, and almost entirely destroyed it before the unfortunate victim to their resentment was found, after being concealed in the house adjoining belonging to a Mrs Strange—an Englishwoman. There can be no doubt that his line of conduct and advice to the Citizens was favourable to the cause of Napoleon; and the popular feeling was at this time so inveterate towards the French, that no interference could prevent the sacrifice of his life. He was dragged into the streets, and mutilated in a manner equal to the most horrible torture—when he expired by the merciful exertions of an old soldier, who had formerly served under him and with tears in his eyes put an end to his dreadful sufferings by stabbing him to the heart.

All Spaniards capable of bearing arms have enrolled themselves as a Militia, to defend Cadiz; and they form a corps of about 6,000, at least double that number having joined the Armies. In its utmost extremity perhaps few places are more calculated for resistance from the nature of its situation—the narrow neck of land, which stretches several miles to the Isle of Leon by a causeway, having been cut through in various places on the approach from Spain. The Town is extremely clean, well built, and well paved, and from the harbour is very beautiful—all the windows having painted balconies. The population is estimated at about 80,000.

CHAPTER IV

GIBRALTAR AND GRANADA

February and March 1809

THE first piece of intelligence we learned on our return from Seville was the death of Sir George Smith; and Mr Arbuthnot called to request, as a mark of respect, that we would, with Major Browne and himself, accompany the body round to Gibraltar in the "Viper," gun brig, for interment—and to this we readily assented, as did also Mr Mackinnon. Sir William Ingilby and Captain Pickering set off next day to Gibraltar by land; and we waited until the 10th for a good wind—when, on going to embark, we found that two Englishmen (Messrs Bailey and Knutzen) had hired three horses to go by land to Gibraltar, and could not proceed as one of them was just attacked with an intermittent fever. The Spaniards were determined to make them pay an exorbitant price for these horses; and on that account I agreed to take the bargain off their hands, and was, after some persuasion, followed in example by Galton and Mr Mackinnon. Mr Arbuthnot had the care of our trunks, and embarked; and we proceeded on horseback through Isola and Chiclana, and arrived at night at Veger—a small town amongst the mountains, and situated on the summit of one commanding an extensive prospect.

The next day our route lay entirely through woods and wilds—where we expected to be robbed by the numerous banditti which infest these mountains: our fears were not very great until about mid-day, when we discovered the quarters of some dead men hung up in the trees by the pathway through the thicket. After this horrid sight we could not entirely dissipate our fears, till we arrived at the top of the Cork Wood from whence we had a most delightful view of Gibraltar. At night we arrived safely at Algeciras, opposite to the Rock; and here our accommodations were tolerably good. Next morning we took our passage in a boat that was going over to Gibraltar with part of the mast of a ship in tow. It blew hard; and the men would not cast off the rope attached to the timber, according to our wishes, as the sea increased. Being just about to land, the spar (or mast) struck the boat and, swamping her, we made our entrée in the garrison wet to the skin. Here we could almost have fancied ourselves in England again; and we spent the evening very agreeably in company with Sir William Ingilby, and Captain Pickering—who on their journey had narrowly escaped being murdered in the Cork Wood.

At Gibraltar we see the instruments of Death and War in their greatest perfection and prepared to keep off any, the most numerous and formidable, enemy. The neutral ground is a sandbank, 900 yards across from the Bay to the Mediterranean, and about two miles long. On this space it is computed that a bird could not live if all the guns which bear upon this large piece of ground were fired at once. The "Lively" frigate has just come in with the dreadful information that the "Viper" gun brig foundered in a gale on her passage: poor Mr Arbuthnot, Major Browne, and every soul has perished. Hence we must all stoop to fate! Galton and myself, only, represent the original Falmouth party of five; yet we pursue our travels to more remote Countries.

The height of the Rock towards Spain and the Mediterranean is 1439 feet—the greatest part of it quite perpendicular. Perhaps there is no precipice that we know of so abrupt, unless it be a part of the Table Mountain at the Cape of Good Hope. There are 607 mounted and loaded pieces of cannon, with the 48th, 57th, and 61st regiments, besides Artillery companies and two battalions of Veterans —making a force of 5,000 men to defend Gibraltar.

Having spent two or three days very pleasantly at the Garrison, Sir William, Mr Mackinnon, and ourselves got into a small boat to visit Malaga—distant about 60 miles. Galton, being a little seasick, stayed upon deck—whilst we three crept into a low and dirty cabin at night. It was quite dark, and the Spaniard who steered us was singing. Hearing this man say something about "il Signor perduto," I imagined Galton had fallen overboard; and starting up without recollecting where I was

—being half asleep at the time—I stunned myself dreadfully against the top of the cabin. Sir William and Mr Mackinnon, hearing the noise, started up likewise and received the same injury. Next morning Galton helped us all out of the cabin, with most horrible headaches—indeed so serious as to detain us some time at Malaga. We lodged at the house of two poor Frenchwomen, whose husbands were merchants, and had both been murdered a week before because they were Frenchmen.

17th February and following days we bathed in the sea, and—having visited a ruinous Genoese castle, and the Cathedral on the 20th—set off next morning together on horseback towards Granada, and after travelling five leagues slept at Velez Malaga. Six leagues, the following day, brought us to Alhama, accompanied by three stout ill-looking muleteers on foot. The night passed tolerably well; but in the morning, whilst mounting our animals, one of the men tied a bag of oily putrid fish to the saddle of Galton's horse, who, putting it aside, so enraged the muleteer that he drew his knife and swore he would kill us all—when I snatched the fish out of his hand and dashed it into his face, at the same instant desiring Conrad (Sir William's German servant) to present his blunderbuss at him, which with threats of death soon made him disarm and throw away the knife. At 3 o'clock in the afternoon we reached the Posada del Sol at Granada. The whole of the road we had travelled over is scarcely passable in Winter, and the country is not at all interesting.

The Alhambra or Moorish temple of Granada is a striking ruin; yet those who have described it have embellished it somewhat as to its beauty or grandeur. The City of Granada is said to contain about 50,000 inhabitants—a trifling number in comparison to what it possessed when under the power of the Saracens; as about the year 1490 it contained 400,000, was three leagues in circumference, and was defended by 1030 towers and 100,000 men. It is situated on the side of a most beautiful and extensive plain; and to the North of it, at about the distance of three leagues, are the highest mountains in Spain—the Sierra Nevada, a chain of mountains higher than the Pyrenees. According to Don Joseph Rodriguez, the Picacho di Vileta is 11,309 feet, and the Carro de Mulhaser 11,585 feet, above the sea[1]. They are primitive mountains and consist of Mica, Slate, Gneiss, Clay, and Serpentine. The summits are covered with perpetual snow. The first and second regions are clothed with lofty Cedars, and vegetation ceases at the height of about 8,000 feet —where the snow commences. These mountains have a beautiful and fine effect from Granada—particularly by moonlight. A constant thawing of part of the avalanches gives rise to the Guadalquivir.

[[1] Or rather, 11,148 and 11,421 feet respectively—the highest peak in the Pyrenees being 11,168 feet. F. D. S. D.]

I prevailed upon Mr Mackinnon to accompany me part of the way—which he did at 5 o'clock next morning. To ascend the mountain, we passed through woods and rocks; and—prepared with a bottle of laudanum, nails in my shoes, a hammer and stick—I took leave of my friend and the guide at the beginning of the snow at mid-day, when they returned to Granada. The object of this undertaking was to explore the original formation of the mountain, as I perceived near the summit a part of the rock exposed like a small precipice. After the first three or four hours in climbing through the snow, with a burning sun over my head—which I kept cool by a piece of ice in my mouth—with feet and body almost frozen from the repeated falls in the snow—sometimes 10 or 15 feet where the footing was false—the frozen region gradually became harder, and occasionally would bear one foot, sometimes both—until about the fifth hour, when it was perfectly hard and firm ice. Now it became steeper and more abrupt as I crawled up a ridge of the mountain chain, breaking holes with the hammer at long steps from each other for my feet. Had it not been for the opium, which I took every ten or fifteen minutes, I might have been hurled down the steep upon the ice with dreadful velocity for many miles—as it appeared—into the bosom of the earth, or into a valley of eternal winter. Still resolved to proceed, I pushed forward as the evening advanced, knowing that it would be moonlight;

but clouds collected, and with difficulty I could just distinguish by my watch that it was 9 o'clock when I attained the foot of the wished for granite precipice. Here—within one hundred feet of the highest part of this chain of mountains—I rested and took more laudanum. Now the most awful hours I ever witnessed began. Darkness prevailed below, and thunder shook the rocks. There was some light above from an obscured moon. The lightning played into the hills beneath on all sides, and set fire to the woods in several places—adding grandeur to the scene. The situation of an individual on this elevation, and at such a time, is too difficult to describe. I was kept here by the lightning until 2 o'clock in the morning, and, on descending, narrowly escaped being shot by some guerillas who met me alone and examined my passport—which luckily I happened to have in my pocket. At 10 o'clock in the morning I breakfasted with my friends at Granada—bringing back a piece of granite, and an empty bottle of laudanum[1].

4th March.—We left Granada and slept that night at Loja, having desired to return by a different route. It was necessary to halt for the next evening at Antiquera; and here Galton and Mr Mackinnon, having walked a short distance out of the town, were seized and marched back as prisoners, but were shortly afterwards released. The next day

[[1] This use of laudanum as a stimulant is noticeable. To a child of the writer it proved fatal. F. D. S. D.]

brought us safe again to Malaga—where, after two days, Mr Temple, the author, also joined our party. Lieutenant Blacquiere, who commanded an English gun-boat, politely offered us all a passage to Gibraltar. It blew a perfect hurricane the whole day. However, he was obliged to sail with his despatches, and we embarked—to the great astonishment of the Spaniards. This gale of wind brought us safely to Gibraltar, completely wet through from having shipped so many seas; for it was necessary to carry a press of sail—or in going against the current we must have been swamped. We were all tied with ropes on the deck to prevent being washed overboard.

The Garrison Library is a great resource to travellers, as we ourselves found it—also the entire examination of the rock, and St Michael's cave, a vast cavern full of such large stalactites that the antiquity of the world is calculated from the time that they must have taken to form. The rock consists of hard, compact limestone; and in the crevices are found the bones of large apes, and other animal remains embedded in argillaceous and siliceous earth. I was fortunate in procuring some remarkably fine specimens.

CHAPTER V

TETUAN AND MALTA

March to June 1809

WE formed a plan of visiting Africa with Sir W. Ingilby, Mr Mackinnon having left him and gone back to England. Mr Temple and Serfatti, a Jew whom we took as interpreter, embarked with us in a Tetuan bullock boat on 28th March. Two large sharks followed our boat from Gibraltar to the Bay of Tetuan—which the superstitious sailors assured us was owing to our having a person on board who certainly continued in an epileptic fit the whole way. Tetuan is about six miles from the sea; and the houses are all white, with flat roofs. Part of the chain of Mt. Atlas runs near to it; and the number of inhabitants is estimated at 16,000—although it was a more important place for some years after the Moors were driven out of Spain.

We were lodged in a tolerable house belonging to a poor man and his Portuguese wife—who we heard had since been murdered—and the next morning waited on the Governor, to whom at the same time it was the custom to make a present, with which we were already provided; and Serfatti, after making numerous strange gestures and prostrations, laid it at the feet of the Governor and his scribes as they sat on their Divan. We presented 2 lbs. of Green Tea and two small loaves of white

Sugar—which was considered a liberal offering. By this gift we obtained two Janissaries to preserve us from the people, who would soon insult and destroy a Christian not protected by the Moorish guards.

On returning from the audience with the Governor, a meagre looking dog attached itself to us, and we encouraged the poor animal—which some Moors observing desired our interpreters to inform us that we had better not have anything to do with the dog as he had only five days to live, having been poisoned a month before. This was a good opportunity of witnessing the truth of the extraordinary stories we had frequently heard about persons having been poisoned who were to die at a particular time, however distant. We fed the animal well, although he did not eat much, and left him in the court of the house in which we lodged: he died at one o'clock on the day named by the Moor, much emaciated, and apparently without pain. I opened the stomach, but could not detect anything wrong there; and it was so extremely offensive from the heat of the weather, that I could not proceed in the dissection. There are several accounts of poisons, the preparations of which were kept secret—as for instance the water named Toffana, after an Italian woman who invented it: this poison proved fatal without leaving any suspicious appearance in the body after death, and was very slow in its operation—producing long fever, vomiting, etc.: Hoffman and G. Melin believed this water was composed of Crystalline Arsenic in a very diluted state. A poison called the Succession, or poison of the Marchioness of Brinvillier, was invented by St Croix, who made it for this lady to effect the impious murders of her father and brothers: physicians were of opinion that this dreadful poison was composed of Acetate of lead and Arsenic acid —they judged this from its bringing on death so gradually.

Our object in Barbary was to visit Fez, the Capital of Morocco—eleven days' journey in the country; but it was necessary to send a messenger to demand of the Emperor permission to proceed. During the first few days of his departure we amused ourselves with shooting in the neighbourhood. In one of these mornings Sir William shot 20 quails and 5 partridges; Mr Temple killed a young eagle on Mt. Atlas; and I shot a poisonous serpent as he was swimming towards us across the river Emgashetabaz —a Moorish word meaning "the road of the bushes." To our great disappointment our messenger returned and informed us it was not the Emperor's will that we should proceed.

Caravans of camels daily arrive from the interior of Africa: we counted 500 in one continued line, and all fastened together. Here we could have purchased oranges at the rate of a thousand for a dollar.

6th April.—It rained all day. Whilst at dinner, the adjoining house fell in and buried two little

Jewish girls, besides injuring many others. This day I was attacked with a very severe headache, from having walked in the sun without an umbrella, and had much fever. Finding it must increase to delirium, I gave directions for my treatment, and passed several days in total oblivion. I was indebted to my friends for my recovery. Their exertions were indefatigable; and they kept iced water constantly applied to my head, brought from the snowy regions of the neighbouring mountains in skins.

On the 17th, being somewhat better, we proceeded towards Tangier on horseback. Having travelled most of the day, and my being totally unable to advance farther, we pitched our tent near a village of Black Moors. Here they had good fresh milk and butter; and all made a good supper excepting myself. We slept part of the night, whilst the guards watched to keep off the wild beasts by lighted fires. Several lions we heard roaring amongst the rocks and jungles near to our tent. It is a very common occurrence for hyaenas to attack persons even in the town of Tetuan; and young lions may be purchased here for a few dollars each. The next morning we purchased of one of the inhabitants the skin of a large lioness, which was brought to us just killed. A Moor entertained us with some serpents which he twisted round his neck and hands, declaring that it would be instant death for anyone to touch them but himself. I attempted to snatch one out of his hand, having observed their teeth were drawn; and for this temerity he would have shot me, had it not been for the interference of the guards.

Our party arrived at Tangier in time to dine with Mr Greene, the hospitable Consul. Next day Mr Greene procured a boat for us to cross the Straits to Tarifa in Spain. It was an open Spanish bark with eight men who were intoxicated, and carried a dangerous and heavy sail in honour of us as Englishmen—'for,' said they, 'it is impossible to be drowned when we have on board those who command the Seas.' Sleeping at Tarifa—where we could not prevail upon our interpreter to land, as Jews are not tolerated in Spain—we resumed our places in the boat next morning, and soon arrived again at Gibraltar. A few days afterwards Mr Temple proceeded in a merchant ship to London.

Sir Wm. Ingilby, being acquainted with Captain Lumley of the "Hind" frigate, obtained his passage to Malta in that ship. Galton and myself were so fortunate as to have an invitation to pursue our travels up the Mediterranean in the "Hibernia," 120 guns and 960 men, Captain Robert Neave—who had padre Gill on board. He was one of the Junta of Spain, and was going on an embassy to Sicily. The ship was ballasted with a million and a half of silver in dollars and bars, for the use of the Austrian and Sicilian troops. Having dispatches for Lord Collingwood, we joined the Fleet off Toulon; and the finest sight we ever saw was

18 sail of the Line going at ten miles an hour under bare poles in a violent hurricane, each ship keeping its exact situation as we ran down to Minorca. Amongst a thousand souls on board our floating battery there was only one man in the hospital—so good is the health of the crew, owing to cleanliness, good food, and constant exercise. One sailor fell above a hundred feet overboard; they regained him, but it was long before he shewed signs of life.

Having passed with considerable danger the Squerks Rocks, where the "Athenian" 74 was lost, on the 11th day the Island of Gozo appeared in view, our vessel having had an unusually quick passage. The entrance to the Harbour of Valette in Malta is extremely narrow; and on the 23rd May 1809 we entered it in the evening, and observed with astonishment the wonderful fortifications from the deck—especially the Castle of St Angelo, which, having five tier of heavy artillery, effectually protects the mouth of the Port.

Next day we found accommodations at the Britannia Hotel in Valette. Civita Vecchia in the centre of the Island has an elegant Cathedral furnished with damask and gold: it contains some very beautiful Mosaic work, and a fine picture of St Paul who was shipwrecked on this Island. Under the East end of the Cathedral is the vault commonly called St Paul's Cave, the earth taken from which is said to be an antidote to the poison of venomous serpents. The Catacombs are curious and extensive excavations, of great antiquity: they are very intricate, and have served at different periods of History to secrete the living, as well as sepulchres for the dead.

Mr Corner's collection of vases, taken chiefly from tombs in Sicily, is extremely interesting, and consists of the produce of above 40 sepulchres. This gentleman possesses great historical information, and much urbanity of manner—having been many years in the Navy, in which he frequently distinguished himself: he has the office of Captain of the Port. Mr Corner, with Mr Tracey of the "Hibernia," took us to see the foundations of the Temple of Proserpine, and also of Hercules—where there is a ruinous statue supposed to be Omphale, and a few other fragments which shew considerable sculpture.

Sir Alexander Ball, the Governor, who had been extremely kind to us, gave a grand assembly on the 5th June, in honour of his Majesty's birthday; and here we had an opportunity of meeting with the most distinguished personages of different countries who were then in the Island.

6th June.—The "Hydra" frigate, Captain George Munday, arrived; and I had an opportunity of enjoying the society, for two days, of my old friend and schoolfellow, Lieutenant William Radford of that ship. The time between this and the 16th passed very agreeably in the society of the civil and military inhabitants of the island. At 9 o'clock in the evening of this day Fahrenheit's thermometer stood at 82°, the sea in the harbour being at 71°.

CHAPTER VI

MILO, SMYRNA, EPHESUS

June and July 1809

ON the 19th we embarked in an American schooner (the "Dolphin"—Captain Le Bree)—paying 50 dollars each for our passage and board to Smyrna—and set sail with a convoy of 34 ships under the protection of the "Wizard" brig of war (Captain Ferris). Our expedition until the 24th was much retarded by calms: for two days we lay within a few leagues of Sicily, watching each night the pale lightnings that played round Mt. Etna, and the blue sulphurous glimmer issuing from its volcano. Towards evening the clouds gathered around, and the sun disappeared before his usual time in the thick firmament. This foretold a change of wind; and so it happened—for a good steady breeze kept up during the night.

Next morning seven of the convoy were missing: towards close of day, however, they again joined us—when the clouds a second time collected and we had a most awful exhibition of lightning. One time the Fleet appeared all on fire; now it streamed as if on a particular ship; at another time it resembled a ball of fire dropping upon the waves; and it repeatedly surrounded every part of our own vessel. This storm was attended with very little rain. The thermometer stood part of the time at 93° in the shade. Many Flying-fish were seen during the thunder, probably avoiding the dolphins which pursued them.

29th June.—We passed the promontory of Taenarus, celebrated for its cavern, and the Island of Cerigo, the ancient Cytherea. On our left we observed a Corsair at anchor behind the little island of Cervi, and above this some extensive ruins in the mountains of Matapan—which we believed to be those of Marathonisi and Gythium.

Towards evening we had a fine view of Milo, and Antimilo—the latter inaccessible and abounding with wild goats—also of the Ananes (very dangerous rocks). The wind changed to N.E., and with difficulty the ship was brought to anchor in the Port of Milo. Having landed, we proceeded to the old city—which is quite ruinous, although a few inhabitants still occupy some of the houses: the ancient walls bear the marks of great waste and decay. It is four miles from the present town, which is situated upon one of the most elevated parts of the island: it is a singular place, as are also its inhabitants: the females wear very short petticoats, and four or five stockings on each leg to make them thick—which are here considered more elegant. The incursions of the Algerines, as well as the plague, induced these few hundred people to neglect their former low situation—the Old City—for this elevated one.

On the foot, and at the side next the sea, of the hill on which the present town stands, are many very interesting remains of a most remote period. Here we could distinctly trace the extent of a large amphitheatre; and many beautiful marble columns are seen amongst the ruins. There you observe walls of an immense thickness; and the cement by which these stones are held together appears to brave the waste of time better than the hard stone itself. The catacombs of Milo are seen many feet below the surface of the sea—hence proving the encroachment of the waters. About 20 years ago one side of the rock on the Southern part of the island gave way, and above 100 acres of stone fell into the sea: although close to the land, it disappeared for ever. This shews the excavating power of the waves undermining these small remains (the islands), probably, of a former continent. The Harbour of Milo was originally the crater of an enormous volcano, and in its history, with the mineralogy of the island, is most curious.

5th July.—We plainly distinguished Cape Doré, and the island of Zea, having passed Serpho and Thermia. On our left, at a distance, the isle of Aegina was clearly seen, but too far off to distinguish the Temple of Jupiter. Many of our Fleet now parted convoy, and proceeded to their various destinations amongst the different islands. The Temple of Minerva at Cape Sunium was very distinct through the telescopes.

6th July.—Passed Andros, Scyro, Ipsera, and Scio, and were becalmed between the island of

Mitylene (ancient Lesbos) and the Asiatic shore. The scenery on each side of the Gulf of Smyrna is most enchanting, wild, and grand. The town, situated at the head of this—crescent-formed, white, very extensive, and broken by small clumps of cypress trees—becomes a most beautiful picture.

Here we landed on the 8th at the hospitable mansion of Mr Werry, the Consul General, and found the plague very prevalent in the European part of the town. The worthy and intelligent Consul takes the greatest pleasure in making every one happy around him. Mrs Werry had retired to Bournabat, a neighbouring village, to avoid the plague. Whilst at dinner with our host, who was waited upon by three Armenian servants, a musket was discharged close to the window—when Mr W. exclaimed "I hear he has killed another"; and we were then given to understand that a janizary was there stationed to shoot the cats as they appeared coming out of the next house, in which all the family had died of this dreadful disorder, excepting a poor infant of two months old which was the only living creature in the house that has escaped: it had been heard to cry, and was found upon the cold corpse of its mother, who must have been dead several hours. Cats are the only animals that communicate the plague to different parts of Smyrna. This large city contains about 90,000 inhabitants.

At 6 o'clock the next evening (9th July) we set off for Ephesus, it being impossible, on account of the intense heat, to travel in the middle of the day —a janizary, interpreter, and guide, with ourselves, all on horseback. During the night the guide mistook the road, which he lost in a forest: here for many hours we wandered about, until fortunately coming to a burial ground our track was again known, to the great terror of our janizary—who discovered that by this error we should have to pass a particular part of this cemetery which was haunted by some supernatural being. He examined his pistols, and holding one in his hand rode a little before us in the greatest dismay. At the exact moment he passed a particular spot, described to us by the interpreter as we were approaching it, a large white animal about the size of a wolf darted across our track; and he instantly discharged both his pistols at it without effect, and declared it was well known to be supernatural, as no one had ever yet been able to shoot it. The dead bodies are covered only with a foot or two of earth—hence that dreadful stench which arises from these bodies of the departed. The jackals come down from the mountains; and here for the first time we saw a whole herd of these animals escaping as we approached, and quitting their prey that was left exposed in putrid and disjointed quarters.

At day-break we halted, and were obliged to sleep under a tree—Mahometans never allowing Christians or, as they call us, Infidels to enter their houses unless they have a Firman from the Sultan.

The day was not so hot as usual; and, it being possible to proceed, we dismounted at Ephesus late in the evening. Here, being a good deal tired, our first wish was to sleep; but we were prevented by a gazing multitude, from the village, of Turks and Greeks. A mat was then spread, and a boy in petticoats with two men and their guitars danced for our amusement and their own profit. It would have been impossible to help laughing, had it not been for the very grave countenances of some older Mahometan barbarians.

Ephesus was once the Athens of Ionia. It is recorded that the Temple of Diana was in length 425 feet, in breadth 220 feet, in height 60 feet. Here most certainly the foundations of a building nearly of the above dimensions may be traced. We are told that it was built 356 years B.C., that it took nearly 200 years to complete, and was afterwards destroyed by fire. Many beautiful columns of granite and Verde Antique now lay amongst the ruins: eight of the latter 60 feet long in single stones were removed some centuries ago to the Mosque of St Sophia in Constantinople (where they now support the Cupola) in good preservation.

The more diminutive relics of many buildings and temples are seen at Ephesus: but tradition does not so easily distinguish them. Over the gateway of an old Genoese castle, built of still more ancient remains, we remarked some beautiful Altorelievos in marble, representing the death of Hector and the giving up of his body by Achilles to Priam. Had this been found at Troy, how much more valuable would it have been! We offered the Governor 1,000 piastres for this piece of sculpture, but in vain. Several vast pillars of granite in an old mosque at the foot of the town are worth observation. The Caystros runs close by the village: part of it is still navigable down to the sea—a distance of four miles, which is chiefly a morass formed by the deposition from mountain torrents. The Carduus Benedictus upon the ancient walls, and the Cucumis Agrestis, grow abundantly at Ephesus.

Spending a whole day on this interesting spot, we journeyed again towards Smyrna, but varied the route by visiting the site of Colophon, where the ruins of a temple called Clarius are scarcely distinguishable. On the 2nd day we again found ourselves at Smyrna amongst the plague—which has increased, 400 persons having died in our absence. I had now an opportunity of watching the progress of this disorder in several English sailors, who having been on shore had caught the infection. I also visited the Armenian and Greek Hospitals, where numbers were dying daily of the Plague.

14th July.—At 7 o'clock in the evening we set off by land to Constantinople, and arrived at Magnesia at half-past five in the morning. During the night several large caravans of camels passed us on our road. The examination of the Town, with the interval of a few hours' sleep, entertained us till the evening—when at 6 o'clock we again mounted our horses, and passing over an extensive plain arrived at 2 o'clock in the morning at Palmont—a poor hamlet. Here resting till 9 o'clock, the day being somewhat cooler, we resumed our journey and in 8 hours came to Yallambai—a village of no interest: we remained here a few hours, and then proceeded to Pendahora, and about the third hour of the road from thence came to the most romantic and beautifully grand scenery that had occurred on our road, reaching nearly to Sursenluk—our abode for that night. We observed several very large serpents in this beautiful forest, and great numbers of land tortoises. We passed near to Morlech, and sleeping, after a dreary ride, at Meekalets[1] on the 20th, at 4 o'clock in the morning entered an open boat, and sailing for 12 miles down a most delightful river found ourselves in the Sea of Marmora or Propontis at about 9 o'clock. Here, in our little bark, we were tossed about until late the next evening—21st July—when to our great joy we anchored at Constantinople, and proceeded the next morning to a comfortable inn.

[[1] Mualitch—on the east bank of the Suserlu Chai—some 40 miles west of Brusa and 15 miles from the Propontis. F. D. S. D.]

CHAPTER VII

CONSTANTINOPLE

July to September 1809

A LETTER of introduction from Sir W. Ball procured us much kindness and attention from our ambassador, Mr Adair, with whom we dined, and in the evening visited the Swedish Minister, Mr Pallen, who is considered the first Antiquarian in the Levant. We witnessed the departure of about 30,000 men on their way towards the Danube to meet the Russians: they were variously dressed and armed, and appeared to be without discipline. The Grand Vizier marched with them.

July 26th.—We attended Mr Adair to an interview with the representative of the Grand Vizier. It was curious to observe the luxuries of a Grand Turk: as he reclined on his couch, no less than four clean napkins exquisitely worked in gold lace were separately thrown over his knees in the space of a minute—for, if he did but touch one, another was immediately presented. He took a small quantity of coffee—when a slave on one knee offered a vase of burning aloe root, the fumes of which his Grace gently wafted towards his silvery beard. Our ambassador exchanged papers with him, and was allowed to sit in his presence.

Mr Adair procured a firman to make the tour of all the principal mosques; and attended by a numerous guard of janizaries we first visited the magnificent one of St Sophia. The interior is spoiled in appearance by the great number of ropes suspending lamps from the top of the Cupola, which is adorned with a curious Mosaic work: the whole has a shabby and dirty appearance. Here we observe the eight columns of Verde antique which were brought from Ephesus, each 60 feet high by 7 feet in diameter: all the small supporting columns are of the same kind of marble. In one part of the gallery some of the smaller pillars are out of their perpendicular; and it is probable an earthquake will ere long destroy the whole. The pavement of the gallery is worthy of observation, being composed of immense stratified marble stones, each exposing a surface of 15 feet by 7 feet. The height of the dome from the top to the floor is, I believe, 170 feet; and the length of the body of the mosque is 260 feet.

The Mosque of Sultan Achmet is next in size, and interiorly resembles that of St Sophia, but is infinitely neater; that of Mahomet Pacha is small, but clean; and the mosque called Little St Sophia is neat but diminutive. Suliman is a large and fine mosque: it has a superb mausoleum attached to it which had never before been exhibited to Christians, and the dome is beautifully ornamented with Mosaic work—but the painting is very coarse, as in all of them.

On proceeding to another Turkish place of worship, we came to the famous Tripod—one of the heads of which (fable says) Mahomet struck off with his sword: it is of copper and about 8 feet high, representing three serpents entwined together, and was brought from Delphi. Near to this is the celebrated granite pillar, formerly conveyed from Egypt—but how or by what means is totally unknown: it is raised on four copper supporters on a base which is surrounded by hieroglyphics.

Mr Adair now proposed that we should enter a Turkish Coffee-house to eat Cabob—fragments of fried mutton cut and rolled in pieces about the size of a chestnut. We were obliged to sit on the floor and eat with our fingers out of the same dish, according to the custom of the people. On calling for something to drink, a large wash-hand basin was brought to us, full of sherbet—a liquor made of dried raisins; there was a spoon or wooden ladle for each; and, although not very agreeable to the taste, yet being cold it was grateful. We afterwards returned across the water to Pera, much pleased with a long day's amusement.

On Friday the 4th August, being the Sabbath of the Turks, we were in some degree recompensed after our former disappointment—in not being able to see the Grand Signior—by now witnessing his procession to the Mosque. He passed under our window, attended by janizaries, bostangres, etc.—altogether forming a most striking spectacle on horseback.

A visit to Buyakdere, a beautiful village on the

Bosphorus near to the Black Sea, where most of the ambassadors have country seats, was our next object; and about three hours in an open boat landed us at Marriott's European Hotel. On the way we passed near to the Sultan's Kiosk, where he now resides, and to which place all his ladies are removed from the Seraglio. An extraordinary firing commenced from the forts on the Straits, which on enquiry proved to be rejoicings for the safe confinement of one of the Grand Signior's concubines of a daughter: sixteen others are in daily expectation of giving birth to an heir to the Ottoman Empire. Here we became acquainted with a Mr Keer, who was one of the few persons saved when the "Ajax" blew up off Tenedos. His history of that sad event is most affecting; and he possesses in an eminent degree the true hospitality which characterises our countrymen wherever we meet with them abroad. The garden of the late Swedish Minister commands a grand view of the Black Sea, the Sea of Marmora, the whole of the Bosphorus, the Minarets of Constantinople, and the distant mountains of the Asiatic Olympus. A curious Oak tree at the Prairie near Buyakdere is well worth observation: I suppose formerly a very large stem occupied the centre, and the present immense trees have sprung from one circular root.

10th August.—We crossed the Bosphorus (about a mile wide), with our landlord Marriott, to ascend the hill opposite, and inspect a giant's sepulchre and a very fine view. The marks of a tomb are very indistinct, but the beauty of the scenery fully compensated for an hour's walk under a burning sun: at each step some ruin of former power meets the eye, and the distant shores and mountains enchant the sight.

12th August.—We visited the beautiful village of Belgrade, so much the resort of Europeans from Constantinople—especially in the time of Lady Wortly Montague: near to this place are the celebrated aqueducts—one built by Theodosius, which consists of two tiers of arches and has 30 in the upper row. The largest was built by his sons Arcadius and Honorius: it is extremely long, having 50 arches in the upper tier and 47 below. The supporters of each arch are equal in breadth to the diameter of the arch, and they are the same size: allowing therefore 15 feet 3 inches to each, and the same to each pedestal, will give 508 yards 1 foot —this being the length of the aqueduct without its abutments, which at each end extend 150 yards. The aqueduct built by Justinian in point of architecture far surpasses the others: and it consists only of four lower arches, but has three tiers of them.

August 17th.—On our return to Pera, in company with Mr Muir and Mr Zorab, we examined the cannon foundry, and were surprised at seeing the whole contents of each furnace, without the dross being removed, let into the moulds. From thence we proceeded up the harbour to the Docks, and ascertained that the Turks could in one year furnish sixteen sail of line—amongst which are three first rates and a sloop of war, with eleven frigates.

On dining with Mr Prior, an intelligent Levant merchant, he gave me a fine Scorpion with about 30 or 40 young ones on its back; and these it occasionally devoured when in want of food—in the course of a few days the whole of them disappeared. Having found a Tarantula, we confined them in the same box: they immediately commenced hostilities, and after fighting for two days the Scorpion killed the Tarantula.

Thursday.—Mr Muir and myself took horses and guns, to shoot at Belgrade; and here we slept but little, being disturbed by the horrible noises in the forest, which extends an unknown distance and is full of wild beasts such as bears, wolves, wild bulls, boars, monkeys, jackals, hyaenas, poisonous serpents, etc.; and these when prowling at night create a furious discord. Two bullocks were this night devoured close to the village, and their remains found scattered towards the thicket. The inmost recesses of this prodigious forest have never been explored; and so afraid are the peasants of the wild beasts, that unless in company with many armed men and dogs they never venture into it. There are some good roads along the outskirts of the wood; but the natives will not traverse these after it is dusk.

The desire of visiting unfrequented spots induced Mr Muir and myself to penetrate into the forest.

Being provided with that most useful instrument, a pocket compass, we arrived by 4 o'clock at the beginning of this labyrinth, which it was said no one had unravelled, taking with us provisions for the day. Each armed with a double-barrelled gun, a pistol, and a large knife, we spurred on; but our horses seemed afraid to enter the wood. Having proceeded about a mile, our course was somewhat impeded by an extensive marsh; and here, though everything was still as death, we observed marks of the feet of wild beasts which had been to drink. Soon we heard a piercing scream as of a jackal, as well as the lonely note of the vulture and bittern. The day was particularly well calculated to such a scene: the clouds lowered, and there was not a breath of wind. The thicket entangled us more and more every step we advanced. Having ascended a hill by almost impassable tracks for about three miles, our horses started suddenly—and a formidable precipice down which we had nearly been carried checked our progress. From hence we enjoyed a considerable prospect of hills and valleys covered by this forest; and all appeared one wild wood, except where the Black Sea was just discernible between the distant mountains. We then changed our course, but met no enemies, nor could any burial place be more silent: the wildness of the scenery was truly sublime. Towards mid-day, being fortunate enough to find a spring of water in rather an open spot, we dismounted and, though expecting to be attacked every moment, regaled ourselves for an hour. We continued to explore the wood, but with the same success, and returned safe to Buyakdere about 8 o'clock at night—to the surprise of all who lived near this formidable thicket.

A few days afterwards we visited the shore of the Black Sea at Doumousdere; and near this we noticed a stratum of coal in the cliff overhanging the sea. About this time Mr Ball and Mr Vaux, whom we had known at Malta, arrived at Constantinople; and in their society we passed many pleasant days. The "Entreprenante" cutter, 8 guns, Lieutenant Williams, arrived in 38 days from England—which is considered a remarkably quick passage—with Mr Ruff the King's messenger.

CHAPTER VIII

ABYDOS, TROY, TENEDOS, SMYRNA

September and October 1809

On 15th September we resolved to return to Smyrna by a different route, and soon after crossed the Bosphorus to Scutari, and taking horses from thence set out for Jebza at mid-day, and reached it at 9 o'clock in the evening. Jebza, the ancient Lybissa, is now but a poor town, and bears very few marks of its former splendour. Near this place and about two miles on the road to Ismid (or Nicomedia), on the left hand side, is the tomb of Hannibal—a vast tumulus without a moat: it appears very much diminished by time and floods, stands in the middle of a plain, and the summit commands a distant prospect of Mount Olympus. Passing this sepulchre early in the morning, we reached Nicomedia at half-past two, and slept here.

The Governor, as is generally the case when he wishes to make the most of travellers, represented the road as much infested with banditti, and advised our crossing over in his boat to Ceramuza—where we arrived in eight hours, and, sleeping in a caravansary, embarked again in the morning (not being able to procure horses) in the boat to Yallova, about 9 hours distant, and were here fortunate in hiring mules, and passed on to a village called Pasaichia.

We set off early next day. Having travelled about five hours, the wood appeared on fire, and the flames spread over the valley and cut off our retreat. It was necessary now to hasten on with all expedition, the fire before us raging through the thicket and increasing rapidly; and we had just time to accomplish our end, when the whole road which we had just left was in one vast conflagration. Over the smoking embers we observed numbers of roasted serpents, tortoises, and a few of the larger animals. In our way through Gemlik and over the mountains a violent thunderstorm arrested our progress, the rain absolutely falling in such torrents that the brooks were too deep to pass; and we slept at Chieflake—only four miles from Brusa.

Proceeding early the next morning, we soon arrived at a caravansary in the middle of the City of Brusa. Signior Killi, a physician to whom we had an introductory letter, congratulated our arrival at the ancient capital of Bithynia; and we removed to his house.

24th September.—We visited the Mosque of Orcanes, son of Othman, which was nearly burnt to the ground and is now in ruins. It would have been desirable to have entered some of the other places of worship, which are said to be no less than 350 in number; but on account of this time being the Turkish Ramazan, or kind of Lent, no Christians could ask the favour. Brusa contains 37,800 Turks, 4000 Armenians, 2400 Greeks, and 800 Jews—

making a total of 45,000 inhabitants. It stands at the foot of Mt. Olympus, on the edge of a beautiful plain. It is famous for silk, and for its natural hot baths. Fuel is so plentiful here, that the charcoal is made upon the mountain, and left in the ravines—when the torrents or occasional floods bring it down into the City.

The summit of Olympus is said to be more than 9,000 feet above the level of the Sea. On expressing a desire to ascend this, the Governor ordered ten of his horse-soldiers to accompany us as a security against the banditti. In five hours we came to the beginning of the snowy region, and the guides would not proceed. We were gratified with very fine views of the hills near Constantinople, the Lake of Apollonia, etc. On a flat near the summit we found some wretched shepherds with great numbers of immense dogs, guarding a flock of sheep from the wolves, etc.; and Bayracta, our Captain, ordered one of the sheep to be caught, when he exercised his art—that of an executioner—upon it. A large fire was soon made near an excellent spring of water; and the animal, roasted whole, was soon eaten by our party with the greatest relish. Salt was the only luxury wanting; and this was supplied by eating gunpowder—the nitre or saltpetre of which was very grateful. This circumstance surprised the Turks much: they asked if the English always ate gunpowder, and if that made them so formidable in war. The repast was no sooner over than a large wolf appeared at no great distance from us: one of the party immediately fired at him, but the shot took no effect, and he darted into the wood. Mt. Olympus abounds with wolves, bears, wild boars, bulls, jackals, apes, a few tigers, hyaenas, vultures, etc. We were a good deal surprised at seeing large numbers of Martins, or Swallows, in the cold region near the summit of the mountain. The plant Mandragora grows wild here in abundance: the fruit somewhat resembles a small lemon, and the shepherds eating it as a soporific are frequently destroyed—many tombstones mark the spots where these unfortunate persons have died in the above way.

The Governor of Brusa respected our firman or passport from the Sultan more than any aga we had before seen. Signior Killi and Monsieur Arlez—the former an Italian, the latter a French emigrant—were truly kind and hospitable to us. Nouradin Effendi, a rich Turk, was very polite, and requested our company that he might tell us he was a friend of Lord Nelson's. He enquired after the several brave Captains of the Navy; and he was the most hospitable Turk we had met with. He commanded a Turkish ship at the battle of the Nile.

Brusa is much resorted to by the rheumatic and infirm, for the benefit of its natural hot baths. These are circular, with cupolas, and have very little light from a small window which is never opened. The Turks remain an hour or more in these places at a time. The air in these baths is at first extremely oppressive, being the same temperature as the water. You afterwards recline on a divan in a chamber at a degree of warmth between the atmosphere at 76° and the bath at 114° Fahrenheit, with a fountain of water at 60° in the centre; and here a cup of coffee and a pipe add greatly to the luxury of the bath, which altogether occupies nearly three hours. There is a spring at 55°, called Bournabas, which issues by a very powerful stream from the rock in the city; and here is a most delightful retreat for those that wish to cool their grapes or melons in the fountain.

Friday, September 29th.—We parted from our kind friends at Brusa, and set out for the Plains of Troy and Smyrna; and, as the road was much infested by robbers, it was necessary to take another guard besides our own janizary. We therefore desired to have Bayracta—as all the country fears him, being a mute or executioner. There is something very impressive in the extraordinary quiet and silent demeanour of these people. We never saw Bayracta smile: he seldom spoke—and then always in a low whisper. We desired the interpreter to enquire how many people he had beheaded in his time; and to this he made no reply. One of the janizaries, however, told us he had decapitated four persons the day before our arrival.

After passing the greater part of the day over a dreary plain, towards evening we enjoyed a very fine view of the Lake of Apollonia—a large and beautiful piece of water with several islands. Near to its banks there stood an ancient castle (probably Genoese) in ruins; and the dread our guards exhibited by making us keep close together, with our firearms ready to discharge on passing it, gave us to understand this was a favourite haunt of the banditti. The evening was now closing in; and a singular flight of wild fowl, at an immense distance over the Lake—as they turned upon the wing, appearing first white then black—attracted our attention. The setting sun heightened the effect. The moon was past the full; and, as it grew rapidly dark, we arrived on the banks of a large river near Morlech, and found the bridge had sometime before been carried away by the floods. A fire, at no great distance on our left in the wood, was marked by Bayracta as a nest of robbers; and he said it was necessary for us to ford or rather swim across the river—which we accomplished with much difficulty. About two hours after crossing this river (the Rhyndague) we arrived entirely wet through at Morlech—in the dark—and spent a most comfortless night.

30th September.—Leaving Morlech early in the morning, and passing through several small Greek villages, we reached the spot where Mithridates conquered Pompey at Cyzicus. It was formerly an island, but is now united to the mainland by a sandbank: there had been a bridge over this part, but it was destroyed by Mithridates, and the waves appear to have deposited the sand against the ruins of the bridge. We made the best of our way to Artace (Artaki), a town at the end of this peninsula, stretching into the Sea of Marmora. Mr Auzet, a polite Frenchman, to whom we had a letter of introduction from his father at Brusa, accompanied us to the ruins of Cyzicus; and we descended into many of the cellars and ancient chambers. The only inhabitants are innumerable bats—so vast indeed in quantity as to create a strange noise by the fluttering of their wings in these dark abodes. I might add that thousands of them adhered to the roofs and walls of these chambers; and we were obliged to destroy great numbers of them to preserve our faces and candles, at which they flew—to our great annoyance. We discovered nothing else of novelty in these secret cells: the ruins are but little interesting, as far as relates to architecture, nor are they very extensive.

All things in Turkey are contrived with so little ingenuity that even the shoeing of an ass requires three men—one to hold his head, another his leg, and a third puts on the shoe which has been purchased at a neighbouring shop. We constantly observed them cast a horse before they could shoe him. Their ploughs are made entirely of wood, and a man carries it home several miles in the evening as they do in Spain.

Leaving Artace at 10 o'clock in the morning, we

reached Vatiha, or Muchacha, at half-past four—the road having been very delightful by the water side. Proceeding next day over a flat country we had the satisfaction of crossing the river Granicus, but did not observe any tumuli or other marks of Alexander or Darius. At Caraboa, where we remained for the night, are some fine Genoese ruinous fortifications. Next day (October 5th) in four hours we arrived at Kemmer on the coast: here the inhabitants were gathering the fruit, and the women with naked legs pressing out the wine. There are large orchards of the Locust fruit tree, from which the Rachee, or Gin of the country, is made. According to the Governor's account of this place, many murders had been committed on the road by land to the Dardanelles: we were therefore obliged to proceed in a boat. It was four o'clock before the little barque could be got ready. We set sail with a rough sea, but weathered the night, which was extremely dark—there was no object for the Pilot to steer by, except the appearance of a mountain now and then visible from the lightning.

Just as it was day-break we anchored at the ancient Abydos, or, as the Turks call it, Chanak Kalessi: opposite is the Sestos of ancient days. This is the narrowest part of the Dardanelles. It is almost a mile wide, and the current runs two knots and a half: therefore it is impossible to swim bona fide from Sestos to Abydos—exactly facing each other—as Lord Byron found: he drifted about a mile to the South of Abydos. Here we find the strongest forts the Turks possess—there being four castles altogether mounting 400 guns, with some of which they cast immense granite balls of 800 lbs. weight, as our Fleet experienced on passing them during war. Here Xerxes threw over a bridge of boats to pass his formidable army.

The Storks or Cranes have now quitted this country for a warmer climate: they usually migrate to Egypt. Being venerated by the Turks, they build their nests upon and even in the houses. Their sagacity is very remarkable—an instance or two of which was told me by a friend long resident at Smyrna.

"Some duck eggs were placed in the nest of one of these birds, her own being removed, and in time she hatched them. Rising from her nest, she appeared wonderfully surprised at the young ducklings: after some minutes' examination she commenced a loud noise, like a watchman's rattle, and immediately 40 or 50 male Storks flew to the nest and, gathering round her, alternately looked at the ducks and at the female Stork—when they all with one accord fell upon the foster-mother and pecked her to death."

"A female Stork, from an accidental wound, was unable to migrate with the rest, and spent the Winter chiefly in the Consul's house and garden at Smyrna. On the return of the other birds, two of them on arriving went up and pecked at her, as if to reproach her for not accompanying them: she instantly refused food, and hastened her own death by pecking her breast."

October 7th.—We waited all the morning for horses to proceed to Troy. Our Consul, Mr Sabatero, a Jew, did all he could for us, but without success. In the evening it thundered and rained tremendously. In our host's dwelling the windows were all put open; and all the Jews in the town were in confusion, expecting every moment that our Saviour would enter their houses. I was surprised to find how little damage is ever done by the lightning in this part of the World, although so frequent and so terrific. At this place we observed some beautiful girls with long auburn hair and red nails—both occasioned by the Henna, or Lausonia Ramis Inermis of Linnaeus. The custom is so ancient that the nails of mummies are found thus dyed.

Sunday morning, October 8th, we set out from the Consul's; and passing the village Erinkerry, where we commanded a fine view of the Hellespont, we rode on to some ruins called the Temple of Apollo—now a burying place; and here are many beautiful sculptured marbles standing up as tombstones. From hence we passed on to Chibluk, a village hard by—where, leaving our baggage, we diverged from the road for two hours to see an ancient aqueduct originally of beautiful fabric, and situated in the wood: from whence or whither it goes is not yet discovered. We now returned to Chibluk, where we were extremely annoyed the whole night with vermin and filth.

Next day we crossed the Simois, now a small stream, and entered Bournabaschi—the site of the Scaean Gate—and, leaving our horses, walked up to the tumulus of Hector and examined the supposed spot on which Troy braved a ten years' siege. Here, alas! are no traces of ruins or walls: the situation is rocky and uneven and on the borders of the Plain. Having spent several hours in contemplating this interesting ground, and the river winding nearly round the supposed site of the ancient city, we returned to the Scaean Gate, and near to it ascertained that the spring called "cold" was at 60°, and that said to be "hot" at 63° of Fahrenheit—the atmosphere being at 74°. I repeated the experiment frequently with the same results. The tumulus of Oecites—from whence Polites espied what was going on in the enemy's Fleet—stands nearly in the midst of the Plain; and from this we enjoyed a most beautiful view of the whole. This tomb is known by the name of Udjek-tepi, and has never been opened. At Pashaw Chiflik is a long inscription upon a marble sarcophagus. Crossing the Scamander we came to Geni-Cheyr, a Greek town near the tumuli of Antilochus, Ajax, Achilles, and Patroclus. Not being able to procure a boat to visit Tenedos, we went on towards Alexandria Troas, and slept at a place called Gaiaclek;

and at this, as in all other hamlets on the Troad, there are ruinous fluted columns or other marks of former splendour.

A fisherman's boat carried us over in two hours to the island. To have a full view of Tenedos we ascended its highest hill, and deplored the cruelty of the Russians on so delightful a spot. The modern town is in ruins; and the inhabitants that escaped being murdered are not yet returned. Melancholy reflections crossed our joys on viewing the wreck of the "Ajax," 74 guns, "lying scattered in the bottom of the Sea." It will be remembered that this, one of the finest vessels under the command of Sir John Duckworth, took fire the day before he passed the Dardanelles to Constantinople[1]. It is remarkable that the accident happened immediately in front of the tumulus of Ajax: she drifted to the island of Tenedos, and there lies a fearful wreck, most of the crew having perished.

The wind sprang up, and we returned in an hour to sleep at Alexandria Troas, called by the Turks Eski Stamboul (or old Constantinople)—so famous for its extensive ruins. There are many columns here of black granite, which measure 38 feet 7 inches in length by 13 feet in circumference, and are single stones. Several sarcophagi are found here—one of them with a curious inscription. That part, which the peasants of the Country call The Castle, was

[[1] In 1807—in his futile attempt on Constantinople. F. D. S. D.]

by far the most perfect of the ruins, but was entirely thrown down by an earthquake seven months since. The very extensive remains of Alexandria Troas are situated in a wood, chiefly of the Dwarf Oak from which the Valonia of Commerce is obtained. About four miles from hence is a powerful spring of hot water, 146°, called Lidgikummum, arising in a valley that retains the appearance of an extinct volcano. The water contains much iron and copper, and is very saline. An exertion of this subterranean fire might have destroyed the fine remains of Alexandria Troas, as there were no accounts of an earthquake having been felt about that time elsewhere. Here amongst the ruins I caught a thick black snake 5 feet 6 inches long: I drew his teeth, carried him to Smyrna, and he lived some months.

Having travelled all day and passed through Inak, which is rather a large town, we came at length to Byramyteh, and here reposed in the most comfortable caravansary we had met with on our travels. Three hours and a half next morning brought us to a village very much resembling Belgrade, at the foot of Mt. Ida, called Chonchonslu. The mountain is 4,960 feet above the level of the Sea, and this spot is generally the resting place for a day before you begin the ascent. Having advanced for two hours, a spring of water at 66° is found; and the Simois which runs close by it is at 45°. To this fountain numbers of invalids resort, and leave their crutches or parts of their garments as memorials of the benefits they have received. Proceeding up the mountain we continually, where the ground was soft, observed the impressions of the feet of wild boars and wolves, and once some very distinct marks of the large paws of a bear. This Alpine scenery, as following the course of the Simois, is uncommonly grand; sometimes it forms a cataract over immense rocks, and then perhaps hurries into the bosom of the thicket by which this chain of hills is universally clothed. We were nine hours in ascending, and did not then attain the summit by two hours more—in consequence of the snow. There was, however, a most magnificent view of the Plain of Troy, Tenedos, Imbros, Lemnos, and other distant objects. The Propontis appeared like an immense lake; and altogether it was the grandest picture we ever witnessed. We remarked several formidable precipices, and Vultures and Eagles—one of which I shot. Seven hours' descent on the opposite side of Mt. Ida brought us to the village of Abjelik, where we could scarcely sleep from contemplating the wonderful expanse of scenery we had just seen.

Three hours from hence brought us to Adramethium now called Adromitch, a large town with very few ruins. We frequently looked back upon Ida, and were more and more struck with "this wild pomp of mountain majesty!" There is a natural hot bath, 122°, clear and well tasted, near to the town, which may be said to stand exactly at the foot of Mt. Ida. Part of the inhabitants live by hunting, and part by fishing—for a creek of the sea comes nearly up to the town.

The chain of Ida consists of micaceous schistus: there is also a great deal of black granite, of which most of the sarcophagi, columns, etc. are formed, which we find on the Plain of Troy. It has been asserted that all granite found here originally came from Egypt; but this is evidently unfounded, for the whole island of Delos consists of black, and the island Myconi would supply plenty of red or Oriental, granite. In an obscure part of the mountain chain, near an ancient aqueduct before mentioned, is a rock of Verde-antique situated in a ravine between the micaceous schistus. The stone has evidently been quarried here, and might formerly have supplied the numerous columns and other specimens of this mineral observed in Greece, and probably the eight stupendous columns at Constantinople—once at Ephesus.

Changing horses, we proceeded to Kemmar and from thence to Jasmat, and arrived at Bergamo at 9 in the evening of the 15th. Here many ruins, and a Genoese castle built of the marble remains of former temples, cannot but excite the greatest interest. There are several Greek inscriptions on some of the walls; but they are inverted and high up above. Spending a whole day at Bergamo, we journeyed on to Minimin, a small place with a disrespectful Governor—and an extortioner. At four o'clock we arrived again at Smyrna, having finished our travels in Asia—much to our satisfaction. We were greeted by our worthy friends, Mr and Mrs Werry, with the greatest warmth of heart and hospitality[1].

The plague had increased considerably; and by an invitation from the native physicians I had an opportunity of attending and taking charge of several hospitals—the Greek and Armenian ones containing at least 120 patients in each. This was a good opportunity to become conversant with the diseases of the climate; and from constant observation I found the plague was frequently checked by an active practice of which the Medici of the East were totally ignorant, hard eggs and salt fish being the hospital diet. Phthisis is most prevalent. Intermittent fevers, and the Lepra Graecorum, are very peculiar in the Levant. There is a curious account of a dumb woman in the Greek Hospital in Hobhouse's Travels: I witnessed this object with that gentleman, and he made a very correct outline of her idiotic countenance.

[[1] Bergamo is the ancient Pergamon. F. D. S. D.]

CHAPTER IX

ATHENS, ARGOS, DELOS

November and December 1809

2ND NOVEMBER. Messrs Galton, Burgon, and myself left Smyrna on horseback, and travelling for six hours along the coast came to Vourla, and, sleeping here, proceeded next day for ten hours to Chesmee, where the Russian Fleet gained a victory over the Turks some few years back. We suffered severely from the most violent storms of rain, on this day, that had overtaken us on our journey. With much difficulty the Greek Governor was induced to take us into his house; and a dying man in the next room, who expired about midnight, added much to the discomfort of the evening.

About the middle of the day following, a boat was ready to sail with us to the island of Scio; and it was dark on our arrival at an Italian convent—the priest of which received us very hospitably. This island was very interesting as being the place celebrated as the habitation of the Harpies, and for the school of Homer which is about two hours' walk from the town. This consists of seats cut in the rock, of a circular form, with a central piece of stone which has the remains of seven lions carved upon it—and from this it is supposed Homer taught: there is room for only about 40 pupils, instead of one hundred, upon these seats. Other antiquarians believe these remains to have been a temple of the Sybils; since the under part of the rock is excavated, and they might have communicated the oracle through this.

The dress of the Greek women at this island is extremely curious. They are the only persons in the Ottoman Empire who are allowed to wear any green colour. They rouge in the extreme, and look beautiful at a little distance. Passing a group of them we heard several of the shortest girls address the tallest by the name Calypso: immediately the goddess with her nymphs were represented to us in life. Scio is esteemed one of the most fertile of the islands, and particularly in its produce of gum-mastic.

Tuesday, 7th November. Having previously engaged for 300 piastres, or shillings, a sacralever (boat of the country) with a triangular sail, with ten men, to carry us to and from Athens, we embarked in the middle of the day with a strong North wind, and ran down in three hours to the end of the island, where we anchored till midnight, and again setting sail had a dangerous passage of 17 hours to the isle of Andros. Here remaining all night, and the wind becoming foul, we were obliged to steer away to the safer anchorage in the Port of Sera—15 miles distant. The remains of the walls of an ancient Stadium are the only ruins on this island: some tombs have been occasionally opened, and we picked up some very old specimens of vases and pottery. The only inscriptions now existing were found at the Stadium, and carried up to the Bishop's house.

Sunday, 12th November. The winds and waves somewhat abating, we again set sail in the little barque at 7 in the afternoon, and early the next day, passing the island of Zea, entered the Gulf of Athens. Here, the wind failing, it was necessary to ply our oars all night; and we got safe into the ancient harbour of Piraeus at 3 o'clock in the afternoon of Tuesday, 14th November, and in two hours afterwards reached Athens.

This morning had given us very fine distant views of Athens, of the Temple of Minerva Sunias at Cape Colonna, and of the Temple of Jupiter at Aegina. There is no country in the world so rich in natural and artificial wonders, consequently so interesting, as Greece; and none enjoys a more delightful climate. A first view of Athens appears like a dream; and a kind of reverence and awe takes possession of the mind in first contemplating the vast ruins of ancient genius. One of the most conspicuous are the ruins of the Temple of Jupiter Olympius: there now remain 19 columns of the Corinthian Order, each 60 feet in height. The Acropolis of Athens contains many surprising ruins, and from its grand situation commands many views of distant temples and beautiful scenery—as of Salamis, Aegina, Hydria and Thermia more distant, the Morea and the Isthmus of Corinth, Mount

Parnassus, and the Acropolis of Corinth. Lord Elgin's painter, Signior Lusiere, and Monsieur Fauvel the French Consul, were extremely polite in explaining the localities of some temples and ancient buildings of which not a trace remained above ground. There are a few cannon mounted on the Acropolis; and the Turks occasionally exercise their skill by firing at the remaining columns of the Temple of Jupiter Olympius, and thus contribute with the waste of ages to their destruction.

On the 18th November we set two men to work at the Piraeus with spades to find a tomb; and they succeeded in finding one which contained one Patera, and a skeleton. There was also a small serpent—the Amphisboena Alba (said by Linnaeus to be found in the Ants' nests in America)—in this sepulchre alive; though on examination we believe the tomb to have been air-tight.

The next evening about midnight we set sail for Aegina, and in the morning examined some ruins of the Temple of Juno and some curious sepulchres. I here obtained a beautiful votive offering in Terra Cotta, which had been taken from the tomb. The Temple of Jupiter Pamellinus, situated about 15 miles from the Port of Aegina, consists now of only 25 columns; it is 50 feet wide by 100 in length. In our walk we shot some red-legged partridges—with which this island so much abounds, that on particular days in the year the inhabitants scour the fields in great numbers and destroy the eggs.

Having just returned to the town, the clouds became overcast and a very tremendous storm arose, the lightning became extremely vivid and near to us, and the peals of thunder were truly terrific. A pleasant wind setting in, after a second stormy night, on the 23rd November we embarked in a small open boat with three men, and sailed at ten o'clock towards Epidaurus: two hours after leaving Aegina the clouds again collected, and the fury of the Elements obliged us to land in the haunted and uninhabited island of Angistri for an hour—when we proceeded, and arrived with a fine moon at Epidaurus. Our boat had red sails, which are less visible to the pirates.

We passed the night in a miserable hovel, and next day (24th November) travelled for four hours along a most beautiful and romantic vale and reached Liguria. Near this spot are the ruins of a town, many baths—the records of Aesculapius—and an immense amphitheatre with a small one near to it.

On our way to Argos next day we had a fine view of Napoli di Romana situated on a peninsula, with a Genoese castle upon an opposite rock. We saw the ruins of Tiryns, and at a distance the lake or morass of Lerna, famous for its dragon. A large white Vulture came from the mountains and hovered over us for some miles, but at too great a distance for our guns to take any effect.

26th November. We were detained at Argos on

account of the rain, and between the showers visited an ancient amphitheatre, the seats of which are cut out in the rock. Near this is the ruin of an ancient castle which Clarke describes as of Grecian origin. Upon a high rock behind the town is a fortress where the Turks have a few cannon, with which they are almost constantly wasting gunpowder. On examining this at a distance, a drunken Turk fired a bullet amongst us, and we then retreated. No offer of money could gain us admittance to their fortress or Acropolis. During the night we were awakened by some wretches breaking into our house; and, arming ourselves, we rushed towards the spot, but could not overtake them.

At a short distance from Argos are the ruins of the ancient City of Mycenae, the capital of Agamemnon; here also is the tomb of that general, which is of a conical form in the earth—46 feet 8 inches in diameter at the bottom, and 43 feet from the roof to the floor. The celebrated Gate of Lions is still seen amidst the ruined walls; they have lost their heads and are otherwise much injured.

Three hours brought us to Nemea, where are three columns of marble—the only standing remains of this once famous Temple of Jupiter. Near to this are several caves in the hills—one of which may probably have been that of the Nemean Lion, as the rock is of hard limestone and the caverns would not easily be destroyed by time. Four hours more brought us to Corinth: here we applied for permission to ascend the Acropolis—from whence Pegasus is said to have winged his way with Bellerophon to Mount Parnassus—but the Turks refused our admittance. There are numerous ruins at Corinth; and about a mile from the City is an ancient theatre much resembling the one near Seville in Spain. The ancient Sicyon is about four miles from Corinth; and here are the ruins of a castle, besides many remains of Grecian buildings and a fine old amphitheatre. Here we purchased a few coins with the dove upon them—the ancient emblem of the city.

The Governor refused us permission to cross the Isthmus; and we departed in the evening for the Port of Rhetum, and sleeping by a cedar fire passed over in eight hours in a boat to Megara—across the Gulf of Athens. This town is solely inhabited by Greeks, the Turkish Governor having previously been carried off and murdered by pirates. It is situated about two miles from the shore. We observed some foundations of ancient buildings, and bought a few coins with the prow of a ship upon them—the emblem of this City, so celebrated for ancient naval power, the birthplace of Euclid and of Eubulus.

2nd December. We left Megara, and in four hours reached Eleusis, which is half-way to Athens; and here we examined some ruins of fluted columns with Ionic capitals, which were evidently the remains of the Temple of the goddess Ceres—which figure was carried away by Dr Clarke and lost at Sea. About three miles from Athens we observed a sarcophagus discovered by M. Fauvel, who supposed it contained the bones of a priestess of the Temple of Venus which stood near this spot: two or three elegantly formed vases were sent by him to France, which had been taken from this tomb. The beautiful landscape of the Plain of Athens now faded upon the sight, the evening closed in fast, and darkness prevailed ere we reached the gate of the City. Our worthy hostess, Theodora Mina Macri, welcomed our return, and prepared all the delicacies of Athens for supper—after which we enjoyed repose, and dreamed of ancient Greece.

Next day, being recovered from the fatigue of travelling from Megara, we called on our friends, and were happy to find Messrs Ball and Vaux had arrived: the former had just learnt the death of Sir Alexander Ball—his father, and Governor of Malta.

4th December. We walked up to the tomb of Philopapas, which is a very conspicuous object near the Citadel of Athens: it appears to have been either circular or crescent-formed, and is adorned by some alto-relievos. From hence the Stadium on the banks of the Ilyssus attracted attention, and a few minutes' walk brought us to its remains. Here the Gladiators contended for glory; and a Temple of Victory is just at hand to receive the conquerors. The subterranean passage, through which the defeated were driven in disgrace to avoid being abused by the spectators, still exists. On returning to the town we visited the Temple of the Winds, now used as a Turkish mosque: each wind is represented by an alto-relievo figure with wings. There was formerly a weather-cock on the top of this octagon building, which pointed to the emblem or figure from which it blew.

In the evening many Turks and Greeks came for advice—each bringing presents of sheep, fowls, ducks, wine, etc. One Turkish lady came attended by two black female slaves, who supported her train; but in consultation she refused to let me see her face. I obtained more provisions by my practice than all our party could consume, and the Waiwode or Governor offered me 600 piastres (£30 a year) to remain as his physician; and, when he found this would not do, he begged me to feel his pulse every day—though no disease tormented him. Messrs Ball and Vaux, with Signior Lusiere, M. Fauvel, M. Roche, and M. Gropins—the two latter being French merchants—came to spend the evenings at our lodgings.

The lantern of Demosthenes now forms a part of an Italian convent: it is a round tower ornamented towards the top with Alto-relievo figures, which have all been copied and casts also taken from them. Our guide pointed out to us some ruins which he described as a temple dedicated to Chromis, a son of Hercules. It now forms part of a Greek Church. Fragments of ancient sculpture are to be found in several private houses. A quarter of a mile from the City are the remains of the Pnyx, or Court of Justice: Lord Aberdeen cleared away the earth from it, and with some success. The Temple of Theseus consists of 12 Doric columns on each side, and six at the end: the various fights or feats of Theseus are represented in bas relief on the frieze of the body of the Temple, which is within the columns. It is now used as a Greek Church, and its marble walls are covered with painted saints, etc. etc. In the midst of this celebrated monument of antiquity are deposited the remains of the unfortunate Mr Tweedale, who died here about 10 years since: the French consul spoke kindly about our poor countryman, and had made a cast of his features after death. All this day our ideas were impressed with veneration for ancient times.

Now with sorrow I found that my poor worthy friend Galton had resolved to stay in Greece for several months longer: he spared not labour or expense in collecting coins, vases, etc. etc., and determined to visit every remarkable place in Attica. From his knowledge of the French language he soon secured friends in the Consul and merchants—whose fidelity induced them to assist him in every respect, as obtaining money, etc. etc. After this he intended to visit all the islands, and then talked of returning by India.

8th December proving unfavourable, our friend Galton would not accompany us to Marathon—

being resolved to take another opportunity. Mr Burgon and myself, well mounted, set out, and passing two or three hamlets arrived at last on the summit of a hill which commanded this ancient field of contending armies. The sun had just passed over our heads. He shed his light on distant ships at sea; but the shadow of the mountain obscured the interesting plain beneath. We now descended; and the tumuli, which had scarcely been observable, were lost to us in the fog of night. A poor Albanian's cottage was our lodging; and every homely comfort, that could be procured for its daily inhabitants, was obtained for us; fish, olives, and Attic wine were set upon the floor; and the poor natives of the place were astonished at our coming from England to see the ruins of their former grandeur.

We slept in security, and at break of day with hasty steps hurried to the largest tumulus—there to enjoy the finest prospect of the Plain. Perhaps we now stood on the remains of the brave Athenians who fell in defence of their Country against the Persians! Near this tomb are the remains of a small temple; and a very mutilated female figure lies half buried in the morass—probably the statue of Victory. Near this spot I purchased two coins that a poor man had just turned up with his plough.

Hence, reflecting on the ancient battle, we again ascended the hill—having passed over a great extent of the Plain—and in three hours arrived at the famous marble quarries of Mount Pentelicus, which bounds the East of the field of Athens, as it does the West and North of the neglected expanse of Marathon. The vast artificial precipice here is curious, considering the want of gunpowder in those days: the walls of the quarry are cut so smooth from the top, at least for 150 feet, that it appears as if one immense slice had been shaved off. The Greek characters Z A N are distinctly seen half-way up, cut very deep into the marble. The marble of all the temples of Athens is obtained here; and several large blocks roughly hewn are to be seen lying about, which were never used.

With a fine view of Athens and her Olive Groves we descended the hill, and, as the calm evening closed in, rode on to the ancient City, and supped partly on the honey of Mt. Hymettus—telling to our worthy friend the wonders of our excursion.

We now spent several days in contemplating the Parthenon and other remains in the Acropolis—which we seldom left until the sun, concealing himself behind the distant snow on the summit of Mt. Parnassus, threw a gloom over the landscape of the plain below. A thin piece of marble, which reflects the light amongst some ruins and cannot easily be got at, has been for several ages a matter of superstition to the Turks and Greeks. They believe it to be actual fire, but dare not protrude their long pipes into the crevice and attempt to light them.

December 13th. We left Athens to join our boat at the Piraeus, and to quit Attica for Smyrna. Just before embarking we visited the tomb of Themistocles, which has been opened; and the sarcophagus now lies in the water. Here, taking leave of our kind and intelligent friend Galton, with solemn pledges of mutual esteem, we parted; and, throwing ourselves into the boat, he walked back to Athens, and we pushed off from its shores. The breeze favoured our progress; and the Greeks began to sing, to dispel the gloom of approaching night.

We passed Sunium, or Colonna, and its temple, and in the mild haze of morning looked back upon these ruins where Plato taught in better days. Here the unfortunate Falconer (the poet) suffered shipwreck—which in modern history renders the spot more interesting.

But now Athenian mountains they descry,
And o'er the surge Colonna frowns on high;
Beside the Cape's projecting verge is placed
A range of columns, long by time defaced—
First planted by devotion, to sustain
In elder times Tritonia's sacred fane[1].

Falconer's Shipwreck.

We landed at St Nicholas in the island of Tino, and stayed the night at the Catholic Convent—having had a good passage of 18 hours from Athens.

[[1] The allusion is to the temple of Athene, on Cape Sunium—the easternmost promontory of Attica—for a beautiful engraving of which see H. W. Williams, *Select Views in Greece*, vol. I (London, 1829). F. D. S. D.]

From hence we sailed to Myconi, only 15 miles, and in three hours were most hospitably received by the English Vice-Consul and his two lovely daughters—who made us extremely comfortable. Through the civility of the Consul we agreed for a small boat to carry us to Delos the next day—our own captain refusing to take us. The evening was spent very agreeably; and we retired early to bed with the thoughts of visiting the Oracle next morning.

December 16th [starting] at 8 o'clock, in two hours we reached a Maltese ship at anchor under the Greater Delos, to learn the news. From hence we landed upon a small island called St George, with a Church on it; whence, after exploring for half-an-hour, we proceeded to the Lesser Delos—the site of the Oracle and of former splendour. We landed in a small sandy bay; and immediately the extensive ruins of the Temple of Apollo arrested our attention. All the vast columns lie prostrate in rows, and sufficiently mark the former extent of the building. Several ancient altars are lying amongst the ruins; the bull heads of some of them are still evident; some fragments of inscriptions are here found. The Naumachia, or lake where aquatic feats were exhibited, is oval and about 110 yards in its longest diameter. It is nearly filled with mud and earth of many ages, and no doubt conceals numerous images and other treasures unexplored. No one lives on the island to give information; and the crew of a sloop of war would soon clear it.

The ruins of a vast amphitheatre are seen about 500 yards to the South of Naumachia—the walls of the front being formed of immense stones, which are dovetailed and without cement. All about this place on removing the earth a little, we find extensive remains of tesselated pavement. In front of this theatre are some spacious arched vaults, with spouts to conduct water to them. On ascending the hill from hence, we find many square rooms sunk in the earth: they are about 30 feet deep, dry, and well plastered—hence they were probably granaries. A fine spring rises from the highest rock of black granite. The ruins of a small temple are seen at the summit; but the greater part have rolled to the bottom. There were originally four approaches to this temple—one to each aspect, as is seen at the top by the steps cut in the rock; and, if you follow the North or South stairs, you presently come to the precipice, shewing the irresistible effects of time even on this hard mineral. The mosaic is here beautifully seen, and no doubt formed the pavement of the temple or whole summit of the hill. Part of the subterranean caves were probably connected with the promulgation of the Oracles.

Having spent the whole day on this interesting island we returned to Myconi, and—supping with the Consul—embarked at 10 at night in our Sciot boat, and in 14 hours arrived safe at the Convent of Scio, to the great joy of the worthy priests.

Monday, 18th December, we were confined to

the Monastery by the rains. It thundered much, and a smart shock of earthquake was felt. This occasionally happens from its vicinity to the island of Mitylene. Next day we crossed to Chesmee, slept here and also at Vourla, and then with fresh horses and attendant rode on to Smyrna. Towards the latter part of our journey three armed Turkish horsemen reconnoitred us—whom our guide declared had about a week before robbed him and some people travelling with him: he knew them at a distance, and we had time to be prepared with our guns—which we displayed to intimidate them.

There are some very curious optical deceptions, or rather atmospheric phenomena, frequently observable in the Archipelago. Sometimes we perceive a promontory, or headland, as it were suspended in the air: this cannot be owing to a fog collecting at the bottom of it—or the appearance of its rising or altering its position would sometimes happen; and it always occurs when the wind is in the North. Another circumstance, probably of the refraction of objects, takes place occasionally when we observe the oars only of a boat at a distance —and these appear straight up in the air—without seeing the boat itself or men rowing. The phosphorescence of the water is also very great at certain times of the year—particularly about the rainy season, and in the neighbourhood of great rivers: if it is to be attributed to the animalculae, or eggs of fish, we can suppose that these would be brought down in great quantities by such rivers as the Nile, Danube, etc. Water spouts are very frequent in Summer: the sea appears to be attracted by these extraordinary clouds and to meet them in a very curious manner: one of the Smyrna merchant ships once received considerable damage from being close to one when it burst.

CHAPTER X

THE ISLES OF GREECE

January and February 1810

FROM the 25th December we passed the time very agreeably with Captain Ferguson and the officers of the "Pylades" at Mr Werry's. We visited Bournabat, a beautiful village in the neighbourhood, where most of the French merchants have country houses—Mr Hase being the only Englishman who has a villa here.

Captain Ferguson offered me a passage to Myconi, on my way to visit Naxos and Antiparos—the famous grotto of the latter island being the principal attraction. The "Pylades" was at anchor below the castle, on the Gulf of Smyrna; and on the 2nd January 1810 we ran down in one hour in an open boat—a distance of 10 miles—to the ship. Early next day we weighed anchor and, the wind blowing strong, sailed close to the town of Scio to observe a privateer that harbours there. In the evening it was necessary to lay to—the night being very dark and stormy—and the ship rolled dreadfully.

The next morning was ushered in with heavy squalls; and, carrying only close reefed top-sails, we ran down in five hours to Myconi (60 miles). Here I introduced the officers to some of the inhabitants, and they enjoyed a very pleasant day. In the evening a small vessel arrived, which had some clothes etc. on board that I had sent from Smyrna to Tino some time before: we were surprised to learn that she had been 14 days on her passage—that is, delaying at different islands for fair weather. This morning she was preceded from Scio by another open boat of the same kind, which was upset in their view, and—without being able to afford them any assistance—four men, a woman, and two children perished. Mr Colvin, the surgeon of the ship, visited several patients with me—amongst others the wife of the Primate of the island. After supper the officers returned to their ship, and promised to call for me at Syra in a fortnight. They sailed at daybreak.

The only remains of antiquity at Myconi I suspect to have been brought from Delos. The people are lively and brave; and an instance of the latter occurred a short time back, when a French privateer attempted to carry from the harbour a Maltese merchant brig. The old Consul raised 200 armed men and succeeded in beating off the privateer with musketry, and saved the brig. It was in the Bay of Myconi that the brave Captain W. Paget was mortally wounded some years ago in an action with a French frigate, which he took.

6th January—the Xmas day of the Greeks, and a great Feast. It was cold, with a North wind. I had an opportunity, however, of seeing all the girls and women in the town in their best clothes, following the corpse of an old female to the grave. The body was dressed out on an open bier, with short petticoats, etc. The followers sung and laughed as they moved quickly along.

7th and 8th. It was too boisterous to venture out to sea in an open boat. From the loftiest ground of Myconi I had a fine distant view of the islands of Naxos and Paros—the mountains of which are covered with snow. There is no game on the island, which renders a walk with a gun rather tedious. In a ravine I observed a curious fungus—said to be poisonous—like the eye of an ox: on removing the outer skin, which resembled the cornea and sclerotica, there presented itself a gelatinous fluid of dense consistance like the crystalline lens, which dissolved on being boiled; but the interior part, which was like the medullary portion of the brain, became hard and opaque on boiling.

9th January. The wind slightly abating, I set sail and arrived quite wet at Naxos (20 miles) in three hours—having shipped many seas, which nearly swamped our little boat. The Consul—Count Frangoppolo, a Greek—spoke a little French: he received me with attention, and accompanied me to see Colonel Rooke, to whom I had a letter of introduction from Mr Hase of Smyrna. This gentleman (Colonel Rooke) was employed in Egypt, and for some reason ten years ago, disgusted with the Army, retired amongst the Greek islands: he has a small vessel of his own, and lives comfortably. Colonel Rooke possesses a beautiful and valuable collection of coins, at least 500, and is an excellent antiquarian: he died at Cyprus about 1813, and his coins and antiques have been lost. The Churches contain some ancient monuments; and there are some slight remains of a temple of Bacchus, etc. A fine gigantic figure was lately dug up here; but, the head being wanting, it was not easily understood.

11th January. We rode to a Convent 8 miles from the town to shoot Woodcocks, and stayed the night. On our way we passed along a most beautiful and extensive valley—bounded by high mountains, and enjoying perpetual verdure. "Here alone" said the Colonel "is retirement to be found. Yonder ruin points a once civilised country: now silence rules the scene, and gives a pensive mind time to reflect." I was much struck by the manner in which he uttered these words, and found it was his favourite abode.

A few wild deer still browse upon the heights, and the sturdy boar still haunts the glens. Here Nature has been most bountiful. Fruits of all kinds appear naturally luxuriant; and the dispositions of the inhabitants of this island are superior to those of the others. We killed only a couple of cocks, and, as the serene evening advanced, walked back to the lonely Convent of the vale—where, around a fire of Cedar wood and over a bottle of excellent Santorine wine, I obtained much information from the intelligent Colonel Rooke.

In one of the classical mountains of Naxos, called Jupiter, is an immense cavern, said to be more extensive than that of Antiparos. Leaving the Colonel to pursue another day's shooting, I procured asses, candles, ropes, and provisions, for the subterranean excursion, and—quitting the convent at 7 in the morning—came in one hour to the charming valley of Philota, whose beauties have been mentioned. The snow had fallen on the mountain below the mouth of the cave, which rendered it difficult of access. In about two hours of ascending I overcame all obstacles, and—candles being prepared—entered the dark abode, and pursued the way with danger. At about 100 yards from the entrance, the cavern became too lofty for a few candles to distinguish its roof: huge fragments of rock presented themselves below, and water dropping from the roof alone interrupted the stillness of the place. The guide and my Greek servant now became much alarmed and determined to return; and their fears increased the more I attempted to persuade them to follow me. This being the case I secured my own candle in my hat; and taking the guide's light in one hand, and that of my servant in the other, I marched slowly forward—leaving them to pursue the pale reflected light of day behind me. About 200 paces forward on a progressive descent I stopped to get a stalactite, and, striking it with a hammer, was much startled at the immense noise produced by such a slight stroke in this vaulted

Labyrinth. The numerous echoes gave some idea of the extent of the cavern. The candles now, from drops of water falling upon them, being reduced to one, induced me to return, to respire with much more freedom the mountain winds.

From hence about 14 miles brought me to a curious tower, called by the Greeks Chemeros. It is 94 feet in circumference, its present height 56 feet; but the ruins prove it to have once been of much greater elevation. Built of white marble and without cement, it stands about two miles from the sea on the E. and by S. side of the island. It was probably a watch tower. On my return I picked up some specimens of Emery stone, found only on this island, and used in England for polishing glass, etc. I could not find any of it in the matrix, but plenty on the shore in detached pieces. The greater part of the mountains consist of marble—which is not so good or compact as that of Paros. About five miles from the town is a hill consisting of a very fine micaceous iron ore, or spicular iron not stratified.

13th January. Having taken leave of Colonel Rooke, in whose society I had had so much pleasure, I returned to the town, where the Consul had on previous intimation procured me a boat and three well-armed men to cross to Paros—about four miles. Just on embarking, another vessel arrived which brought some disagreeable news about the pirates of Naussa—the capital of Paros, and nearly opposite to Naxos. This information immediately deprived me of one of the guards, who said he could not fight against fifty to one. The other savage wretches grasped their blunderbusses, and said they would proceed with me. My servant then became very much alarmed at my continuing the journey, and was about to leap from the boat again on shore; but, on my pointing the gun at his head and declaring I would shoot him if he attempted to depart, he sat down again in the bottom of the boat.

A good breeze landed us in an hour in a creek of Paros, between the village of Marmora and Naussa. The boat immediately returned; and my guards with difficulty procured asses to cross the island to Paroekia, to avoid Naussa. Passing by some of the stupendous marble quarries—for which Paros is so celebrated—late in the evening, and being much gratified with them, I arrived at Paroekia, and with difficulty procured admittance into a Greek convent at 9 in the evening—having been four hours in crossing the island, and less fatigued than my three men who rode upon asses.

Having supped upon olives and eggs, I procured a boat and eight men to row me over to Antiparos—five miles—and got there at midnight. The town is a mile from the shore and well fortified with high walls, etc. etc. The dogs barked at our approach, and the place was soon in an uproar; the people, taking us for greater pirates than themselves, appeared at the parapets with arms; and it was not without long explanation that we were admitted within the fortress. The Governor enquired how many men I would have to attend me to the Grotto; and on hearing them talk of 30 or 40 I declared that 10 were sufficient, and that I would pay for no more. Ropes, ladders, lights, etc. being procured, I set off for the cavern, and counted no less than 43 men —most of them armed—in my suite.

Proceeding for nearly three hours up the hills, we came to the entrance of the famous grotto, and at four o'clock in the morning entered its subterraneous saloons. In the beginning it presents an awful appearance: large stalactites support the entrance, which soon becomes narrow, and darkness prevails. With the help of rope ladders, the first obstacle is soon got over—a perpendicular descent of about 30 feet—and then, holding by a long rope, you walk down a ridge inclining to a great angle, and darkness and depth obscure each side. Cautiously passing down thus for about 200 yards, and hearing stones and broken stalactites —displaced by each footstep—rolling into the abyss, you arrive at another precipice. Here you climb down an old rope ladder left there, fastened to a large stalactite, by Lord Elgin: it is about 40 feet, and then you are happily at the bottom of the cave. All the candles and torches being held up, you are filled with amazement at the wonderful appearance; and, gazing on these grand resplendent and snow-white columns, you tremble at the vast and secret works of Nature.

There is a good account of this extraordinary cavern, and a beautiful view of it, in the Voyage Pittoresque of Choisseul Gouffier, plate 36, p. 72, tom. 1. Paris 1782. The stalactites are of that kind of carbonate of lime called arragonite, and the variety of the crystallisation is very curious. I brought away some differing much in this respect —the generality of them being radiated from a hole in the centre which does not contain any fluid: indeed a peculiar dryness prevails in the upper halls or chambers of this cave. The resemblance of the crystals to a variety of vegetables is particularly striking.

Having, after much trouble and dispute, rewarded this nest of pirates, I arrived again at Paroekia at mid-day, but could not procure a boat large enough that would venture to carry me to the island of Syra—for the sea ran very high. I was therefore detained here all day. Having resumed my quarters in the Greek Monastery, I tried to sleep for two hours—when, being refreshed, the interior of the Churches was the object of research. In the chapel of the Convent are several ancient inscriptions. In a private house I was shewn a beautiful figure with a perfect inscription; but the owner demanded 100 piastres (£5) for it, which was more than I chose to give.

15th January. At 7 in the morning I left Paros, without regret, for Syra—though I was sorry to part with my faithful guards. The crew of this boat consisted of four men. Having quitted the land, and discovered one of them to be a Frenchman, I alarmed him by saying he was my prisoner, and that I should consider him as such when I got on board the "Pylades," which was to meet me at Syra. This man, it then appeared, was about to join a French privateer at that island, and worked his passage over in my boat to get to his ship. Great indeed was my astonishment when in four hours I landed at Syra and found that Captain Ferguson had only six hours before fought and taken the Privateer in the very harbour of the island: he had left all her crew upon the land to the number of 240, after having killed about 50. On my landing they understood I was an Englishman, and I thought I saw revenge light up all their countenances. The Vice-Consul, a Greek, was much alarmed for his own safety, as well as mine.

I passed the night in meditating an escape, and Tuesday morning hung very heavy upon me. I sent George, my Greek servant, to the water side —where the sailors were selling what they had preserved from Captain Ferguson to the inhabitants of the island. By mingling with them as a native, he presently understood that a man was stationed at the corner of a street to shoot me if I stirred from the Consul's house. He joined in the common detestation of me, and was then told in confidence by one of them that I was to be dragged from the house at mid-night, and to be robbed and murdered. On hearing this I dispatched him to hire a boat of a man who was of the French party, that it might be believed by them I was about to quit the place at midnight—which, however, of course was not really the case; for, very fortunately for me, the Consul's son and two men were fishing on the other side of the island, and had a boat there.

At about 8 o'clock, in a Greek dress, I passed over the roofs of some houses with the Consul—deeming it more prudent to leave George, the better to deceive the people—to evade the street, and thence along a rough and dangerous road of about 7 miles to the little sandy bay—where my friend saw me safe in his boat. In four hours and a half I was sheltered in the hospitable Convent at Tino: the kindness of the venerable Fathers of this establishment will ever be remembered with gratitude, and made such an impression on my heart as never to be forgotten. Their religion and habits differing from the Greeks', they depend upon a limited society and an excellent library for happiness. My servant arrived the following morning, with a long account of the search that was made for me by the Privateer's men, who could not believe I had left Syra.

One of the altars from Delos is seen at the door of the Swedish Consul at Tino. There are 66 villages on the island: one of them should rather be called a large female convent, being walled round. The Greeks and Catholics are at almost open war; and last year the latter had ten men killed, and the others nearly as many. The Turks have consequently taxed the island very heavily. Silk stockings at about six or seven shillings a pair are made here. A great number of young women are annually sent from hence to Smyrna and Constantinople as nurses. Some of them marry and return to live at Tino: most of them have learned cleanliness, needlework, and the care of children from the Catholic families. The proportion of women is much greater than that of men: the latter are chiefly fishermen and petty merchants, and having acquired an independence retire to one of the mountain villages to live in idleness. From the hills of Tino we have a fine view of Myconi, Delos, Syra, Jura; and Naxos, Paros, Antiparos, Serpho, Siphanto, Thermia, Zea, and Nicaria form a more distant prospect. The roads of Tino are extremely bad, and there are very few antiquities: the tombs of the ancient inhabitants are not even found. Above the town are some remains of an aqueduct. There is a cave on the cliff of the shore, about a mile from St Nicholas, worth exploring. No Turks whatever reside at Tino—which makes it safe even in time of war with Turkey: hence Mr Froaddin, the Russian ambassador, now lives here, whilst his countrymen are in irons and working as slaves at Constantinople.

20th January. I embarked in an open boat, with my servant, a poor woman, and two men—prayers having been previously offered up at Mass for my safety, and the worthy friars giving me their blessing. We sailed in company with two other boats. I persuaded the pilot to keep in shore about a quarter of a mile from the coast; this he was the more willing to do on observing two strange boats with red sails hovering near the island, and here we escaped the fate of one of our little convoy—who, as the evening advanced, was chased by the pirates and carried into Jura. The other stood out to Syra; and we, coasting the island at midnight, arrived at Banarmo, an excellent little port on the North of Tino. A Church and three uninhabited huts occupy the beach; and two large Greek ships here lay in anchor. Our appearance in the dead of night alarmed the crews, who took us for plunderers and were at their quarters to receive us. The moon shone resplendent as we took possession of the Church, five yards long by three wide. Next day I walked to the villages of Pyrgo and Plataea (four miles), and spent the day in the house of a Greek whom I had known at Smyrna. The harbour of Banarmo is well adapted for the exportation of marble for grave stones. At night I slept again in the Church, and could only get olives and oil to eat. We now resorted to the necessity of drawing our boat out of the water, to prevent the waves destroying it.

23rd January. Walked to the town of Anasteria, which is the highest point of Tino. There being no probability of the wind changing, I set out on the 25th to pay a visit to the friars of St Nicholai—a journey of six hours—and passed first through Plataea, then through Anasteria and the highest ridge of the island. Mr Vitali, the English Consul, and the fathers of the Convent, were delighted to see me; and I slept there. Next day, to vary the tour, I kept along the shore for four hours—then going straight up the mountain to the village of Guardiana, which contains about an equal number of Greeks and Catholics. My servant here recognized an old female acquaintance, who shewed us every attention. From hence one hour brought us to Anasteria; and, being fatigued, I slept in the house of a poor woman who had fresh milk and cheese.

In a creek about three hours from Banarmo are some ruins of a small temple, of an inferior kind of Verde Antique. A sort of stone table was found here some years ago, and sold at Constantinople for two thousand piastres (shillings). They may be the remains of the Temple of Neptune, mentioned by Anacharsis. The foundations of an ancient Genoese town are seen about a mile from it. My residence being now known at most of the villages on the island, I exchanged medicines for provisions, and lived tolerably well.

4th February. I left Banarmo, and after a tedious passage arrived at Ipsera, and with much thunder and lightning. The Church here is worth seeing; it contains about 25 little gilt models of ships, representing the vessels which belong to the island; and they say that St Antonio was a sailor, to whom the

Church is dedicated, and hence their voyages are more propitious. Ipsera is one of the chief trading islands in the Archipelago. The nearest point to the Isle of Scios is about five miles. Eggs are only one para each (half-a-farthing), corn very dear as at the other islands. Butter sells for two piastres and a half per oke (2½ lbs).

A large ship appeared in the South this morning coming from Malta, and great crowds of women watched her from the hills in hopes of seeing their husbands and sons. The isle of Ipsera, with the others which build ships, procure their timber from the forests of Vili Pashaw on the Morea, and their charcoal from Nicaria—which abounds with underwood. The only Frank (European) resident here is a French doctor in the service of the Greek Governor, who pays him £20 a year. The men on the island are haughty; the women rather handsome, and they do not wear trousers or drawers as the others all do in these islands. The wine of Ipsera is very bad, and contains a great deal of resin, which lines the inside of the skins in which it is kept.

The 11th, at 9 in the evening, I embarked with 40 Maniots from the Country in the South of Morea, and many other passengers. We were becalmed all night, and with much tacking and rowing anchored at 3 in the afternoon at Fogi on the Asiatic shore in the Gulf of Smyrna. The voluntary swimming of some camels from the mainland about 300 yards amused us on the voyage.

Having slept at Fogi I set out at 8 next day overland to Smyrna (12 hours), and passed over a picturesque country to my place of destination, where I arrived at 8 in the evening, and found poor Lieutenant Branch of the "Pylades" had, in an engagement with a Privateer, received a dreadful wound in the leg—which made it necessary to amputate it. A very strong earthquake occurred at midnight, and increased Lieutenant Branch's sufferings much: several persons were crushed to death by the falling of some houses.

CHAPTER XI

SMYRNA, MALTA, ENGLAND

February to August 1810

17TH FEBRUARY. The "Frederickstein" and the "Pylades" being ordered to cruise, I embarked as Doctor to the ship in the latter—to give Mr Colvin, her surgeon, an opportunity of remaining with Lieutenant Branch on shore. We anchored at Partridge Island in the Gulf, and spent several pleasant days in fishing and shooting. From hence we passed close to Scio, and were driven by stress of weather to anchor at Mitylene (Lesbos) in the harbour of Sigri. This island is as volcanic as Milo, and rarely a week passes without earthquakes. The harbour is much exposed; and on the 23rd, amidst a dreadful sea and incessant squalls, we followed the "Frederickstein," steering for the North of Andros. But she, sailing better than us, reached the passage between Andros and Long Island before it was dark; whereas we, being overtaken by the night, were obliged to stand off the land till morning—when we ran down towards Myconi at 12 knots an hour.

24th February. Reaching the passage between Myconi and Tino early in the morning, and under the Lee of the island, we went on shore, and found Galton at Mr Vitali's. We had much pleasure in relating to each other our adventures since we had met. We stayed two hours at Tino; but I could not persuade my friend to accompany us, when we joined our ship and stood towards Siphanto. All night and next day we were becalmed between Delos and Syra. At length we arrived off Milo, and there learnt that the "Frederickstein" had two days before steered towards Cerigo. We now anchored at the volcanic island of Argentiera. The town is small, but well built and walled round. A Turkish frigate is lying here to watch the pirates. The strata on the North side of the island are most plutonic; and the firing off a cannonade under the cliffs produced a fine effect, and hurled down tons of lava, cinders, etc. into the deep. Having paid our respects to the Turkish captain, who received us with a salute, we passed over to examine the island of Polino. Next day we got between Milo and Argentiera, and a strong wind carried us up to the Gulf of Athens. We anchored in the harbour of Piraeus, and found Lord Byron and Mr Hobhouse here visiting the remains of Grecian splendour. Captain Ferguson gave them a passage in the "Pylades" to Smyrna—where we found the "Frederickstein" had arrived much injured, from having been on shore in the Gulf and disabled for three weeks.

I embarked again in a few days with Captain Ferguson, and we visited Athens once more, also Hydrae, Napoli, and Castro, the ruins of Hermione, and the town of Razeni or Tiryns, the ancient walls of which are considered one of the wonders of Greece.

March 24th. Arrived once more at Smyrna, and found Lieutenant Branch much recovered. Mr Werry, Lord Byron, Mr Hobhouse, and Captain Nourse, dined with us on board the "Pylades." Next day Captain Nourse gave a dinner to the Prince of Nevaid and Count Hartoff, who were going to join the Spaniards, and had never before been on board a man-of-war. They were saluted, and the yards being manned greatly surprised them.

The Chameleon is very common upon the trees about Smyrna. I kept one about 10 inches long; it was very docile, and I remarked a peculiar glutinous secretion from his mouth—so tenacious that a fly when placed upon his tongue could not extricate itself. When irritated it changed suddenly from a grass green to black, and was frequently speckled and blue and brown.

19th April. Captain Bathurst, of the ship "Salette," returned from Malta, bringing the intelligence of the death of Lord Collingwood.

We bathed several times a day; and on one occasion, in swimming from the shore to the "Frederickstein," I touched a Torpedo or Gymnotus Electricus, which produced such a shock that I had the greatest difficulty in saving myself.

I now embarked with Captain Nourse in the "Frederickstein," and again visited Athens for two days, and Milo, Cerigo, and Coroni—in which latter place we found a French privateer that had taken an English merchantman within the rules of neutrality. The Governor refusing to give the ship up induced Captain Nourse to cut them both out—which we effected with the boats after a slight resistance, and the loss of about 20 men on the part of the enemy and several of ours wounded: the prizes were sent to Malta. Next morning we fell in with the "Confounder" gun brig—Captain Vallobray—and her convoy for Smyrna, and all put into the harbour of Modari. Here we find a very superior town to Coroni; and the Consul is a Turk who expects to be well paid for every civility he shews to strangers. It gave us much pleasure to find Sir W. Ingilby was a passenger in the "Confounder," and we enjoyed his society for two days. When we sailed for the coast of Africa—first passing close to Maina or Cape Matapan, and Taenarus—the weather became very foul, and we again put into Milo; and afterwards visiting Delos, Tino, and Scio, we once more got back to Smyrna.

Saturday, 12th May. Here I found that Galton had sailed for Malta, on the Sunday before, in a Tunisian vessel. Captain Nourse had now occasion to go to Malta, and kindly expedited the day of sailing that I might the sooner again join my friend. In tacking about against the wind on Tuesday morning we got aground in the mud—opposite to the castle in the Gulf of Smyrna—and with difficulty got the ship off again, after starting our fresh water.

It was therefore necessary to supply our loss, and we anchored at Scio for that purpose. Here we found the Consul's flag hoisted half-mast high, and understood that his wife had thrown herself into a well in a fit of jealousy.

May 22nd. We visited Cerigo, and gave a letter of introduction to Captain Mackalister of the 35th, who commands here. Upon this ancient island of Venus (Cythera) some finely sculptured lions were lately found. There are no ruins of temples that attract immediate attention. There is a deep and unexplored cavern—something like the Taenarus cave opposite—and in the same kind of limestone rock.

Wednesday evening we descried the "Kingfisher" sloop of war—Captain Tritton—in chase of three Greek ships, but lost them in the night. At half-past seven p.m. on Friday, 25th May 1810, we observed a most splendid meteor, unattended by thunder, in the heavens, and at 8 p.m. on the 29th May anchored safely at Malta.

Here I hastened to the Lazaretti, and found poor Galton in that sad state almost too painful to describe. He lingered until 3 o'clock in the morning of the 5th June; and his melancholy death made me resolve to return to England as soon as the quarantine laws would permit. I found that he had arrived from Smyrna nine days before in an infected Tunisian vessel commanded by Signor Campanelli: she was laden with cotton. Mr Simmons, a Constantinople merchant, and two Ragusee gentlemen who spoke French, were fellow passengers with him. Such ships should always be avoided in time of plague, as in the Mediterranean they are invariably unsafe. Nothing could exceed the kindness of Mr Simmons, who was confined in the same cell of the Lazaretti with my friend; and Messrs Kerr, Chabot, Cartwright, Dr Franchioli (physician to the Lazaretti) and Dr Thomas (first Physician to the Garrison of Malta) came every day from Valette into the quarantine harbour with provisions and to offer their assistance. A poor Italian priest, who had been upon a pilgrimage to the Holy Land, had rendered all the help he could; but old and debilitated, and within a few days of finishing his quarantine of 60 days, he caught the plague and expired in my presence—the day before my poor friend died—in all the calmness and resignation of a good Christian, giving me in a most heart-rending manner the little pearl cross he had worn in his bosom through all the changes and dangers of his life. The evening of the following day all the guns were alternately fired from the bastions of Malta in celebration of the King's birthday; and the loud roar of cannon shook the Lazaretti, and produced in my poor friend a delirium much too dreadful to think upon. He said at last, after many incoherent sentences, "My heart is disquieted within me, and the fear of death is fallen upon me." I endeavoured to raise him up; his eyes were fixed on mine; a kind of cold bloody sweat dropped from his forehead—and he was dead.

Here then I would close my narrative; but the sequel may interest some of my friends, as I had not yet done with witnessing the misfortunes and death of others. Having, through the goodness of Dr Thomas, obtained a passage in the "Minerva" brig, a prize laden with Elephants' teeth and gold dust from the coast of Africa—that was going to England in the convoy of the "Spartan" frigate—and after laying in £20 worth of provisions—instead of going in the Packet, which would have cost £100—I embarked in the "Minerva"; and we left Malta in number 45 sail, with a favourable wind. Upon the Tuesday the weather changed, and on Thursday we were off the island of Sicily with foul winds and a heavy sea. We stood on to within four miles of Girgenti, and the town of Sciacca, and with a glass could distinguish a variety of ruins. The frigate carried away her jib-boom, and a Greek ship lost her fore-yards in the gales. At night we tacked and stood towards Pantellaria, and next morning again advanced towards Sicily, and stood into the Bay of Menfi. The wind on the 17th became rather more steady; and we coasted the island, having Mazzara—a large town with a Cathedral—in sight. We then passed Marsala on the most Western part of the island. At night we were off the small island of Maretimo, and had one of those dreadful displays of lightning peculiar almost to this latitude. The reflection of the light from the snow and smoke of Etna had a very fine effect.

On the 20th and 21st we were becalmed off Sardinia; and two French privateers came out of Cagliari in the night, and carried off three of our convoy. A breeze sprung up about mid-day on the 22nd; and the "Scout" brig of war, Captain Sharpe, joined us. The "Spartan," Captain Brenton, chased one of the privateers which was following the Fleet, and overtook and captured her. 29th June we made Cape de Gaeta, having sailed favourably since the 22nd. Another privateer was chased, but she escaped.

July 2nd. Off Malaga, and witnessed the disembarkation of Lord Blaney's expedition, which terminated so unfortunately[1]. Next day we passed Marbella, and anchored safely at Gibraltar.

July 9th. We sailed for England, but put back next day on account of bad wind, and anchored close to the Packet—which had followed us from Malta. Mr Wilkinson, of Smyrna, was on board and persuaded me to take my passage in the Packet—as I should have to perform Quarantine if I proceeded home on the prize brig. I paid Captain Bullock £47. 15*s.* 0*d.*, and joined the "Express" Packet. We sailed on the 16th and witnessed the operations of the siege of Cadiz, but did not anchor

[[1] The expedition was directed against Malaga; but the foreign troops, of which the force was mainly composed, fled at first sight of the French, and Lord Blaney was taken prisoner. F. D. S. D.]

here. Two whales off Cape St Vincent kept company with our ship for 12 hours, and we shot several bullets into them. Major Howard, one of our fellow passengers, was very ill with a remittent fever—the effects of Walcheren fever: on the 27th this unfortunate and gallant officer expired.

On the 30th July we arrived safe at Falmouth, and were immediately put under quarantine for having the body of Major Howard on board. With much difficulty we obtained permission to bury him on the sands. The ship's flags were hoisted half-mast high, minute guns were fired, the Captain read the funeral service before the body was lowered into the earth, and every respect was shewn to his remains.

Major Howard had belonged to the 4th Regiment of Foot, or King's Own: he was of an amiable and brave character, and had frequently distinguished himself in the Army. The regiment was stationed at Ceuta; and from his account several of the men were dying daily of the Walcheren fever, the effects of which appeared to be much increased by this climate. He told me he thought he should die, but hoped to reach England before that event—as he disliked the idea of being buried at Sea. The remittent fever in two days from our leaving Gibraltar became a continued one—with great exhaustion, and a naturally emaciated constitution. Nothing would stay a moment on his stomach from the first: even Opium, brandy, Cayenne pepper, bark were rejected. Nature appeared almost exhausted; and low delirium succeeded for two days before his death. Before this, he had frequently expressed his gratitude for the attentions shewn to him, and spoke of dying—in a resigned and collected manner. After the delirium commenced, it continued till within a few minutes of his decease—when he looked round wildly, and gradually became sensible: he recollected me sitting by him, and said in a faint voice "My dear friend, I cannot die without I am turned with my feet towards the East." I called the Captain to assist me; we turned him round; he then beckoned to me; on leaning over him close to his face, he uttered "God bless you"—and his eyes became instantly fixed in death.

By representing our case to the Transport Board, we were liberated from quarantine on the 8th August 1810; and, upon landing, I thanked God that I was safe on England's shore again. On this very spot I had embarked with Messrs Clarke, Adey, Arbuthnot, and Galton—all of whom had perished from the fatigues and dangers of foreign climes. The "Minerva" prize—in which I had set sail from Gibraltar, but had been driven back by bad weather and then joined the Packet—foundered in the Bay of Biscay, and all her little crew perished.

APPENDICES

I

Copied from the Obituary in the "Monthly Magazine" *for October* 1810.

"On the 5th June last at Malta, in the 27th year of his age, Mr Theodore Galton, second son of Samuel Galton Esquire of Dudson House near Birmingham.

"This gentleman went to Spain in November 1808, induced by the impulse of a generous spirit to contemplate the exertions of a people struggling for their liberty. After witnessing the accumulated disasters of the Spanish Nation, he sailed up the Mediterranean and travelled through Asia Minor, Constantinople, and the Grecian Archipelago. Amongst the latter he passed several months, regarding, with the admiration and delight which spring from a cultivated and classical taste, those consecrated scenes of ancient genius. Returning from Smyrna to Malta, he was attacked on his arrival at the latter place by a Typhus fever which proved fatal; and he expired in the arms of his friend and travelling companion, Dr F. S. Darwin.

"Mr Theodore Galton was of amiable and polished manners, and would have proved, had he lived, a manly and noble character. It is remarkable that Dr Darwin is the only survivor of five travellers who sailed together from Falmouth in November 1808, the other four having fallen victims to the fatigues and dangers of foreign climes."

II

Island of Milo.

This is very remarkable in its volcanic formation. Its appearance on our approach is very singular, no entrance to the harbour being distinguishable until you are close to its mouth. The highest point of the island, or Mt. St Elias, is about 800 feet above the level of the sea, and is conical. The summit was formerly a place of observation for pilots, but now for pirates who infest the Archipelago. On the North side of the island, and about half a mile from it, are some basaltic rocks—very curious in appearance, without containing Zeolite. Upon ascending from the harbour to the town we pass over hills and rocks of lava, in which Opal is found, and pumice stone and sulphur, and beds of limestone which has been burnt but still retains many perfect shells which soon absorb moisture and fall to pieces on exposure to the air. In one part of a rock of sandstone, at about the middle of the entrance into the Port, are some singular catacombs in the perpendicular rock—some of them capable of containing four, six, or eight bodies; and they are also seen in the rock 10 or 20 feet below the level of the water. This then is a strong proof that the harbour was the crater of a volcano, as these tombs must have been formed before the grand eruption which gave access to the sea. It occurred to me—on seeing in the chart (which was partly copied from an Admiralty book) that 40 fathoms was the greatest depth in this large basin—that there might be a part infinitely deeper which had been the real furnace of the volcano. I was at great pains in sounding, but could nowhere find it to be greater, except at the entrance. At the West and South sides of the harbour are innumerable hot sulphurous springs, some of them being 125° of Fahrenheit; but most of them rise out of the sand in the Sea a few yards from the shore. They are so numerous that every wave, although it blows fresh, is very warm to the hand. Along with the water a great quantity of sulphuretted hydrogen gas is emitted. The ruins of ancient baths still exist here, and near them an inscription entirely erased except the word "Diagoras." Now, if the grand eruption had taken place since the time of that philosopher (about 400 years B.C.) we should have had some records of it: therefore it is fair to presume that the catacombs are of much more ancient date. I obtained a Greek vase taken from one of the identical sepulchres, which has all the characters of the very earliest period of the Arts. The island is still subject to frequent earthquakes; and probably it was an exertion of this volcano, or that at Santorini, which destroyed one of the principal towns of Candia or Crete with its inhabitants in the year 1809.

III

Coal Strata on the Black Sea.

Near a small fort about 25 miles North of Constantinople, and on the beach of the Black Sea about five miles from the village of Doumousdere (or valley of Wild Boars), is a stratum of coal dipping to the South West. It runs along the shore—sometimes on a level with the water, and at other times appearing in the sandstone 20 or 30 feet above the Sea for an unknown distance. I followed it for several miles along the coast; and the stratum, as is seen on the side of the sandstone rock, is in many parts 6 feet thick—though rock and hills, which lie upon and over this coal, are composed of slate clay passing into sandstone. The strata of sandstone are frequently divided by large veins of a compact argillaceous nature containing Mica and running in the same direction. The coal at the surface is quite woody; but at the depth of two or three feet it loses this appearance and assumes that of Pitch. It does not soil the fingers, and is very light. Two Chalybeate springs arise from this stratum of coal, and deposit much ferruginous sediment. I could find no remains of animals or shells in it, or in the sandstone. The surface of this country is covered by the Forest of Belgrade, which appears to have degenerated for many ages, and is too intricate for a mineralogical survey. The ignorance of the Turks prevents them working here: a Pit or Coal trade might turn to great advantages.

IV

Tino.

Tino is a most interesting island for its mineralogy. The mountains consist chiefly of limestone that affords excellent marble, which is sent to Smyrna and Constantinople for gravestones. In the garden of the Italian Convent is a beautiful vein of asbestos running through serpentine, which imperceptibly becomes a kind of verde-antique: in the state of serpentine it appears stratified, and dips to the West at an angle of about 65°. A rich lead ore accompanies the numerous veins of quartz in sandstone. There is abundance of pyrites on the island, and octohedral crystals of iron.

The schistus at Tino, opposite to Andros, is well calculated for slates—which is not the case with that opposite to Myconi, which is too micaceous. On the North side of the island we find pistaziti in beautiful crystals. Several miles on the shore are covered with a black ferruginous sand. Wolfran also is found at Tino.

V

Letter from Dr Mino, an Athenian physician, dated 1809.

"Constantinus Bariniero, a violenti ira fortique animi perturbatione quandoque paulo ante coenam commotus, indebilitate protinus contractili, sensitivique fibri potentia nonnihil exhausta, concidit. Hinc lipothymia, artuum tremores infirmitatesque, anorexia et tristitia secutae sunt. Ad medicinam confugienti difusiva stimulantia primum, utpote cardiaca operatica, pluribus vicibus pro ratione sumenda; dein amara (kina kina presertim) martialiaque, utpote permanentiora, roborantia, ministrata sunt. Dieta analeptica praescripta. His non ad integrum indicationi respondentibus, frigida balnea instituta sunt, ad animationis revocandos exhaustos spiritus, ut activiora remedia inde fierent.

"His peractis, infirmum corpus, non mediocriter roboratum, se ad solita munera vitae expedit. Hyeme vero facta, permanentis frigoris probabiliter, vi denuo directe debilitata, excitabuntur fibra corporis, ideoque laxabuntur; et gravitati suae nonnihil obediens videtur."

Translation of Latin Letter.

Constantine Bariniero gave way one day, shortly before a meal, to a violent outburst of anger, which occasioned much disturbance in a mind already overstrained; and he thereupon fell down in a state of muscular collapse, accompanied by no little exhaustion of the nervous system. This was followed by a fainting-fit, tremblings and feebleness of the limbs, vomiting, and melancholy.

On his seeking medical advice, diffusible stimulants were first administered, such as those acting on the heart, to be taken in frequent doses at stated intervals; then bitter drugs, especially quinine, and invigorating ones, viz. those of a more durable and strengthening character. A restorative diet was prescribed. As these remedies did not quite respond to the case, cold baths were ordered, to revive the exhausted spirits of life, so that more active remedies might afterwards be applied.

After this treatment his feeble frame, not a little strengthened, returned to the ordinary duties of life. As, however, a Winter, probably of prolonged duration, has come on, and his strength will soon be exhausted again, the system will be first stimulated, and then a relapse will take place; and he seems fairly resigned to his serious state.

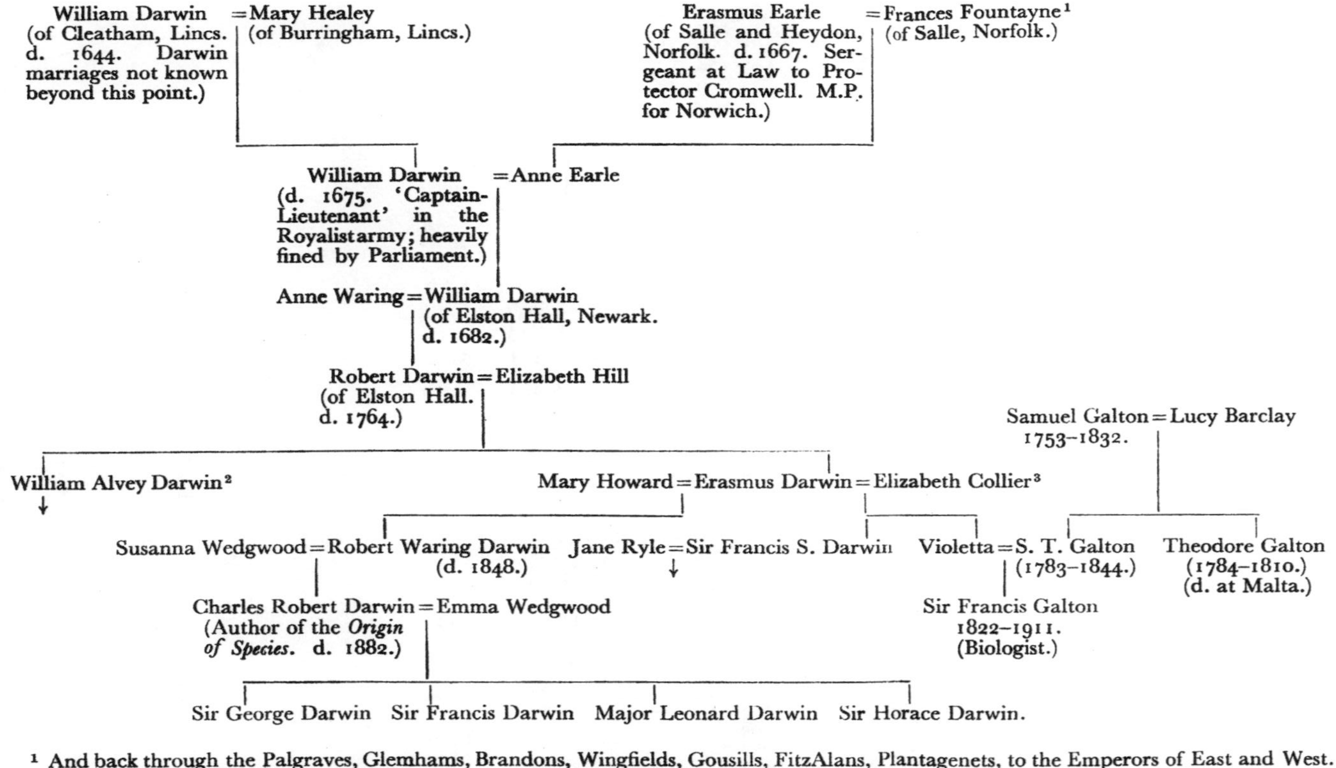

[1] And back through the Palgraves, Glemhams, Brandons, Wingfields, Gousills, FitzAlans, Plantagenets, to the Emperors of East and West.

[2] From whom descends the present head of the family—Col. Charles Waring Darwin, of Elston Hall, who married Mary Dorothea, daughter of the Right Hon. J. Lloyd Wharton by Frances Shafto, and has issue.

[3] For the descent of this lady from Catherine Sedley, Countess of Dorchester and favourite of James II, see Professor Karl Pearson's *Life of Francis Galton*, vol. 1. pp. 18–22. Elizabeth Collier's first husband was Colonel Pole of Radbourn, who led the first British line at Minden in 1759; and from her the present Poles, as well as the Darwins, are descended.

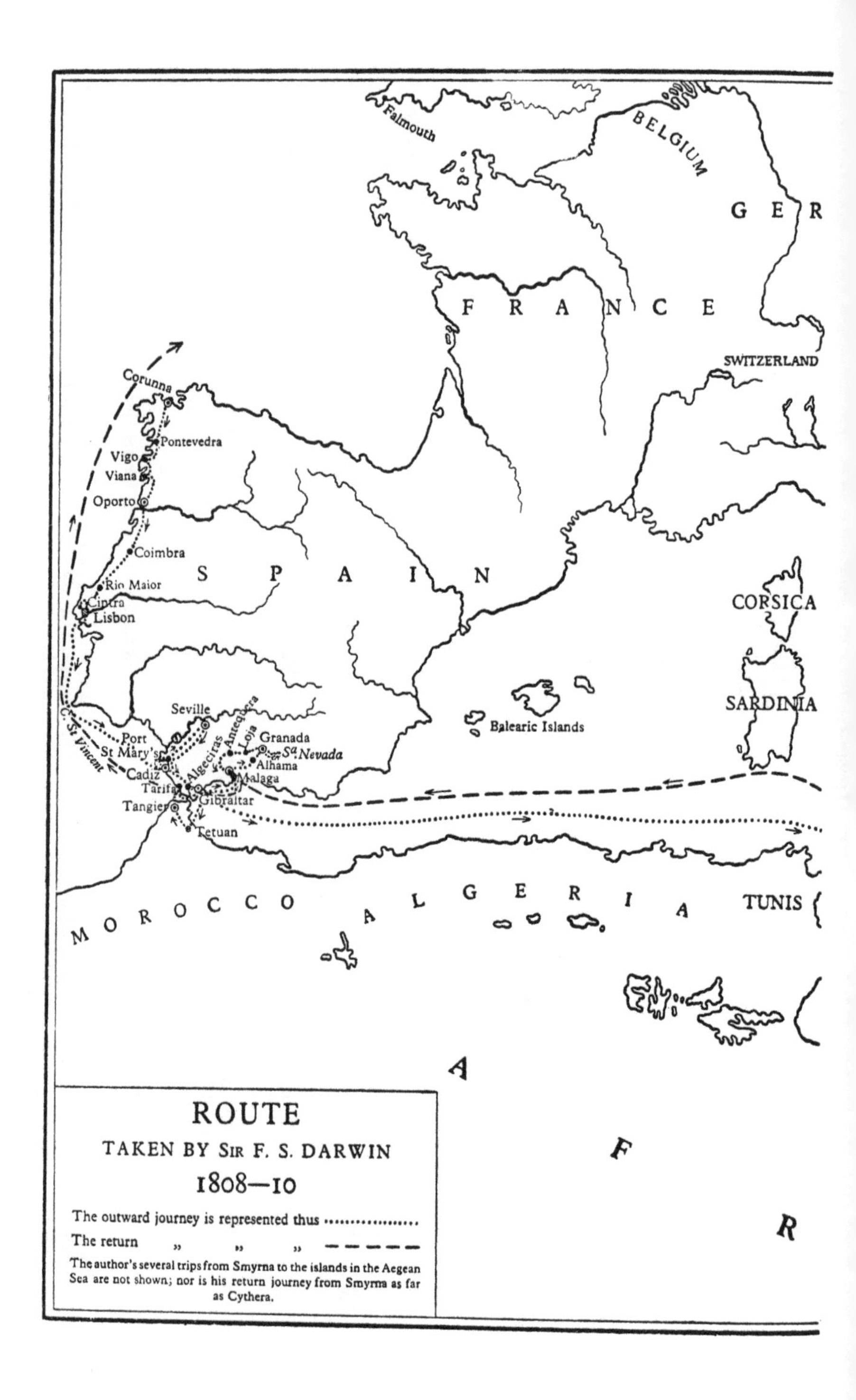

ROUTE

TAKEN BY SIR F. S. DARWIN

1808—10

The outward journey is represented thus ....

The return " " " — — — —

The author's several trips from Smyrna to the islands in the Aegean Sea are not shown; nor is his return journey from Smyrna as far as Cythera.

Cambridge University Press